A STRAIGHTFORWARD GUIDE
TO
FAMILY LAW

DAVID BRYAN

Straightforward
www.straightforw

D0268955

Straightforward Guides

© Straightforward Publishing 2017

British cataloguing in Publication Data. A catalogue record for this book
is available from the British Library.

978-1-84716-669-2

Printed by 4edge www.4edge.co.uk

Cover design by Bookworks Islington

Whilst every effort has been made to ensure that the information
contained within this book at the time of going to press, the authors
and publishers cannot accept liability for any errors and omissions
contained within, or for any changes in the law since publication.

CONTENTS

****

List of cases (page order)

Ch.1

Introduction

The area of family law is a very complex area, multi-faceted, including every aspect of law and legal intervention into the lives, both private and domestic, of those who are related by blood or by association.

Looking at historical definitions of the meaning of 'family' this encompassed a wide group of people who shared the same household. Obviously, earlier interpretations could, in the light of the 21st century, be seen as outdated and oppressive. For example, in R v Inhabitants of Darlington (1792) Lord Kenyon CJ stated that: 'in common parlance the family consists of those who live under the same roof with the pater familias: those who form...his fireside'. Servants were also included in this definition, often living with the same family for the whole of their lives.

Over the years the law has evolved, as law tends to do. By the twenty first century, legal interventions in family life have developed along with definitions of family. Rent Act legislation helped to frame definitions of what was and was not family. In Langdon v Horton (1951) the Court of Appeal refused Rent Act protection to two elderly women who had shared the same house with their cousin for 30 years. The cousin held the house on a statutory tenancy prior to her death. The Court of Appeal held that they had lived together for the sake of convenience and not because they were part of the same family, even though they were cousins.

The following case demonstrates just how much the law has changed. In Gammans v Ekins (1950) the Court of Appeal rejected the claim of a male cohabitant to remain in the family home on the death of his partner. Asquith LJ took the view that either the relationship was platonic and the couple were not members of each other's family or it was not. If the relationship was platonic Asquith LJ believed that to recognize the cohabitants as members of the same family would also require the court to accord the same status to two 'old cronies' of the same sex innocently sharing the same flat. If the relationship were not platonic, Asquith LJ thought it:

'anomalous that a person could acquire a Rent Act protected status by living or have lived in sin, even if the relationship had not been a mere casual encounter but protracted in time and conclusive in character'.

He concluded by saying that to accept a same-sex couple, masquerading as husband and wife, as members of the same family was an abuse of the English language. In Ross v Collins, 1964, a woman claimed the right to succeed to a statutory tenancy on the death of her partner. She had lived with the deceased for a substantial amount of time and was significantly younger than him, 40 years younger, and had looked after him as an elderly relative. Russell LJ ruled that this platonic relationship was not within the definition of family because there was no kinship between the couple. He stated:

'two strangers cannot ever establish artificially a family nexus by acting as brothers or as sisters, even if they refer to each other as thus.......Nor can an adult man and woman who establish a platonic relationship establish a family nexus by acting as a devoted brother and sister or father and daughter would act'.

However, by 1980, the courts had begun to recognize that those living In a stable heterosexual cohabiting relationship could be classified as each other's family. In Watson v Lucas (1980) it was held that a married man, who had left his wife and had lived with the deceased woman in a stable and long-term relationship, was a member of the family for Rent Act purposes.

The above case marked the departure from traditional ways of thinking. Another case which was a landmark ruling, Fitzpatrick v Sterling Housing Association (2000), accepted that homosexuals could be members of each others families. Lord Slynn, in his judgment, viewed the essential hallmarks of a family relationship as a degree of mutual interdependence, the sharing of lives, the caring and love for each other, and the commitment and support for each other. In Ghaidan v Mendoza (2004) the House of Lords further defined family and held that the term 'husband and wife' in Rent Act legislation could be read to mean 'as if they were husband and wife'. It, therefore, included a same-sex partner who had lived with the deceased in a spouse-like manner.

The concept of family and spouse has been further extended since these landmark decisions. In accordance with the Gender Recognition Act 2004, transgendered persons, who have obtained a gender recognition certificate, may marry a member of the opposite sex to that of their newly acquired gender. Prior to the Act this was not the case. The Civil Partnership Act 2004 has also given a quasi-spousal and familial status to same sex couples who register their partnerships. The Marriage Act 2013 has also compounded these rights. (see Chapter two for details of the Act). The law has moved on significantly, as can be seen. However, there are categories of excluded relationships that need further discussion.

Excluded relationships

There are two categories of relationship, which although functionally familial, have only been granted limited legal rights. The first category consists of cohabiting heterosexual couples and also same-sex cohabitants who have not registered a civil partnership. The second category consists of those who live together in the same household as members of the same family but have never engaged in sexual relationships with each other. This is because they are either closely related or because they are close friends who have assumed a personal responsibility for each other but a sexual relationship is considered inappropriate. The increasing emphasis in family law today centers on the needs, rights and overall welfare of children from conception to adulthood. Parenthood is no longer primarily based on marital status and its definition has evolved to cover new forms of biological and social parent/child relationships. More complex means of assisted reproduction present new challenges to legal concepts of parenthood.

In addition, the Children's and Young Person's Act became law on 6/4/2009. The purpose of the Act was to reform the statutory framework for the care system by implementing the proposals in the June 2007 White paper Care Matters: Time for Change. The Act formed part of the government's drive to improve the quality of services and support for looked after children. It includes provision in relation to private fostering, child death notification to Local Safeguarding Children's Boards and the Secretary of State's powers to conduct research and applications for the discharge of emergency protection orders. This Act is summarized in chapter 11, Protection of Children.

Another area which taxes all concerned is the financial implications of relationship breakdown. The emphasis is on the importance of recognizing equality between male and female roles and the establishment of rights in the family home.

Recent changes to the law-The Children and Families Act 2014

The Children and Families Act 2014, which came into effect in April 2014 has introduced several significant changes to family law-summarised below.

The Single Family Court

The Family Court, as set out in the new s 31A of the Matrimonial and Family Proceedings Act 1984, exercises jurisdiction over all family proceedings (subject to a few limited exceptions). There will no longer be a separate jurisdiction for magistrates' courts and county courts to hear family cases. This change is intended to create a simpler court system, allowing cases to be allocated to the judge with the relevant level of seniority to hear the case, with the help of a 'gatekeeping team'. The four levels of judges are lay magistrates, district judges, circuit judges and High Court judges. It is also envisioned that this change will help to reduce delays and will ensure judicial continuity.

These changes have been necessitated by the removal of legal aid for most family law issues, and the delays and problems that have been caused by the influx of litigants in person as a result of the cuts. Although a more simple and streamlined court structure would undoubtedly benefit those involved in family disputes,

Child Arrangement Orders (and presumption of parental involvement)

The Children and Families Act 2014 (the 2014 Act) abolishes contact and residence orders, and replaces them with child arrangement orders in an amended s 8(1) of the Children Act 1989 (the 1989 Act). These new orders define with whom a child will live and with whom a child is to spend time or otherwise have contact. Although these orders will likely have a similar effect to the old orders, the aim is to remove the labels so that parents feel less like they have 'won' or 'lost', and to focus more on the arrangement which is best for the child.

Mediation Information and Assessment (MIAM)

It is now a requirement that an applicant for a 'relevant family application' attends a MIAM before issuing, as set out in s 10 of the 2014 Act. Unless one of the limited exceptions applies, if an applicant has not attended a MIAM their application may be rejected by the court. These changes endorse previous legislative and judicial moves to promote the use of alternative dispute resolution and to use the court process as a last resort. Avoiding the acrimonious court route is clearly a good thing for both the parents and the children involved, and such an aim cannot be criticised. However, this move does also support the theory that the Government is trying to make do with a reduced legal budget, by seeking to reduce the numbers the courts have to deal with.

The above outlines some of the complexities of family law and also illustrates that we have moved from a basic, paternalistic, mode of recognition of family to a more enlightened view, which encompasses much wider concepts such as same-sex relationships. The law dealing with family and family related matters is ever changing and this book brings the reader up to date with legal changes in the new millennium, including the Human Rights Act and issues following on from the passage of this particular legislation in the United Kingdom. In addition, adoption is covered in depth and the Adoption and Children Act 2002 is covered along with a summary of the Children and Adotion Act 2006. The latest developments in adoption law, such as the ability to adopt online are covered.

It is hoped that by reading this book a valuable insight will be gained into this particular area of law. It must be stressed that this is very much an introduction, and is designed to be read and understood by all sections of the community. It will be equally valuable to the layperson as well as the student.

Proposed future changes
Currently under debate is the proposal to open up family court hearings. Under plans outlined by Sir James Munby, pop up courts in public places and also divorce proceedings online could shape the court system in the future. These plans are still very much in their infancy as there is, not surprisingly resistance, particuarly where children are concerned.

****

Ch.2

Marriage and Divorce

The definition of marriage

Traditionally, the definition of marriage has been rather simple, which is 'marriage is the voluntary union for life of one man and one woman to the exclusion of all others'. (Hyde v Hyde 1866). Thorpe L.J. in Bellinger v Bellinger 2001 suggested that marriage should be defined as 'a contract for which the parties elect but which is regulated by the state, both in its formation and in its termination by divorce, because it affects status upon which depends a variety of entitlements, benefits and obligation's.

The Gender Recognition Act 2004 (GRA) highlights the fact that marriage is no longer between those who were born respectively male and female. In addition, the ready availability and ease of divorce renders Hyde v Hyde unsatisfactory as a definition. Further, the Marriage Act 2013, which will be outlined at the end of this chapter, has also changed the definition of marriage.

In the following chapter we will explore marriage as a legal concept. To begin we will look at marriage as defined under the Marriage Act 1949.

For a marriage to be valid, the marriage must have been entered into voluntarily. The parties must intend it to be for life. It must be a monogamous relationship. Both parties must be over 16 and if under 18 must have the consent of those who have parental responsibility. The Marriage Act 1949, as amended by the Marriage (Prohibited Degrees of Relationship) Act 1986 and the GRA 2004 lists those who may not marry.

In order to marry, a person must be capable of understanding the marriage contract. Mental incapacity can render a contract null and void.

The formalities of marriage

The Marriage Act 1949 requires:

- for a Church of England wedding – the publication of banns, a license, or a certificate of a superintendent registrar or naval officer:
- for other marriages – a certificate of a superintendent registrar.

Marriages can be solemnized in:

- a church or chapel of the Church of England
- a registered non-conformist church or other building
- premises approved by the local authority
- any place if a special license is obtained.

Jews and Quakers may marry according to their own customs with a certificate of a superintendent registrar.

Now that the Gender Recognition Act 2004 is in force, transsexuals will be able to marry according to their 'acquired gender'. Section 1 of the GRA permits transgendered persons to apply for a gender recognition certificate from the Gender Recognition Panel which was set up to determine the gender identity of both pre-operative and post-operative transgendered persons over the age of 18. The certificate allows them to acquire a new gender from that of their birth. They need not have undergone gender realignment surgery if it is inappropriate to do so.

Cohabitation

Cohabitation is not a relationship recognized in law like marriage or civil partnership and as a result cohabitees may not have the same rights on the break up of a relationship. The main differences between couples who are cohabiting and those who are not are fairly obvious. A marriage or civil partnership starts when a couple comply with the formalities required for a marriage/cp. Cohabitation begins when the couple start to live together. Although marriage can be proven, it can be open to dispute when a couple started to cohabit, unless there is some sort of formal record.

There is a difference between the children of cohabitants and those of married c/p couples. A husband will automatically be presumed to be the father of a child to be born to his wife (Children's Act 1989 s. 4). That is not so in the case of a cohabiting father. However, if the cohabiting father is registered on the birth certificate he will be presumed to be the father and (since the Adoption and Children Act 2002) automatically have parental responsibility. If the cohabiting father is not on the birth certificate he will be at a significant advantage in that he will need to prove his paternity and even then he will not automatically be granted parental responsibility.

A significant difference arises between marriage/cp and cohabitation if the relationship comes to an end. Marriage can only be ended by a decree nisi issued by a court (Matrimonial Causes Act 1973) while cohabitation can be brought to an end by the parties simply going their own ways. More significantly, on divorce there is the power in the courts to redistribute the property of the couple and to order periodical payments. At the end of cohabitation the only orders available for partner support are declarations as to who owns the couple's home. On cohabitation the court can declare ownership but cannot change it. For wealthy couples on divorce, many millions of pounds can change hands (Charman v Charman (2007) EWCA Civ 503) while on cohabitation the most the court could do would be to order the sale of the house and division of the proceeds (Stack v Dowden (2007) UKHL 17).

Death Can mark another point at which marriage/cp can be significant. If the deceased has left a will there is no difference between spouses and cohabitants. However, if there is no will and the rules of intestacy apply then significant differences may arise. A spouse will automatically inherit all or most of the estate, while a cohabitant will not automatically inherit. All is not lost for the cohabitant who can still apply under the Inheritance (Provision for Family and Dependants) Act 1975.

Surprisingly, there is also a difference in relation to protection from domestic violence. A wife will automatically be able to use section 33 of the Family Law Act 1996. A cohabitant can use section 33, but only if she can show that she has an interest in the property (See section on Domestic Violence).

Nullity, void and voidable marriages.
A court can grant a decree of nullity of marriage. Such a decree declares the marriage to be null and void. This is quite different from a termination of marriage.

A void marriage is a marriage that was never a marriage at all. A voidable marriage is a valid marriage until annulled by decree. As a result the parties to such a marriage must obtain a decree before they are entitled to behave as single people.

There are four grounds for nullity, under section 11 of the Matrimonial Causes Act 1973 (MCA). They are:

(a) that it was never a valid marriage under the Marriage Acts;
(b) that at the time of the marriage either party was already lawfully married;
(c) that the parties are not respectively male and female
(d) in the case of a polygamous marriage entered into outside England and Wales, that either party was at the time of the marriage domiciled in England and Wales. The most common ground used is where one of the parties was already married.

Void marriages and Non-marriages
A void marriage will appear to be a valaid marriage but a non-marriage will not resemble a marriage and will have no legal consequences at all. Thus the court has no power to award any financial order to either party, as it does when the marriage is void. In the cas eof Hudson v

Leigh (2009) Bodey J held that in deciding what constituted a non-marriage, the following (non exhaustive) factors should be taken into consideration:

- whether the ceremony set out to be or purported to be a lawful marriage
- whether it bore all or enough of the hallmarks of a marriage
- whether the three key participatants (including the officiating official) believed, intended and understood the ceremony as giving rise to the status of lawful marriage; and
- the reasonable perceptions, understandings and beliefs of those in attendance.

In de Reneville v de Reneville (1948) a void marriage was described as one which never came into existence. No matter how long the parties had lived together, they can never acquire the status of man and wife.

Grounds on which a marriage is void
The Matrimonial Causes Act 1973, s11 provides the grounds for a void marriage:

S 11(a) that it fails to meet the provisions of the Marriage Acts in that (i) the parties are within the prohibited degrees of relationship.

No one may marry a person to whom they are related by blood or marriage within the prohibited degrees laid down in the Acts. The Marriage Act 1949 as amended by the Marriage (Prohibited Degrees of Relationship) Act 1986 and the GRA 2004 lists those relatives who may not marry. This includes both blood relationships and relationships of affinity:

- father/daughter
- mother/son
- niece/uncle
- nephew/ aunt

21

- brother/sister
- grandparent/grandchild
- half-siblings
- adopted child/adoptive parent

A person may marry his or her adopted sibling, his or her step-child if both parties are over 21 years of age and if the child, prior to the age of 18, has never been a child of the family in relation to him or her. Marriage between a daughter-in-law or son-in-law with a parent in law is permitted if both parties are over the age of 21 and their former spouses are both dead.

(ii) either party is under the age of 16. In Pugh v Pugh (1951) Pearce J stated:

'According to modern thought, it is socially and morally wrong that persons of an age at which we now believe them to be immature and provide for their education should have the stresses, responsibilities and sexual freedom of marriage and the physical strain of childbirth. Child marriages, by common consent, are believed to be bad for the participants and bad for the institution of marriage. Acts making carnal knowledge of young girls an offence are an indication of modern views on this subject. The remedy that Parliament has resolved for this mischief and defect is to make marriages void where either of the parties is under 16 years of age'.

A person domiciled in England cannot evade the law by marrying in a country where the law is different.

(iii) the parties have intermarried in disregard of certain requirements as to the formation of marriage.

One case that highlights this is Gereis v Yacoub (1977). The parties went through a marriage ceremony or a purported marriage ceremony at a Coptic Orthodox Church knowing that it was not licensed to carry out marriages under the Marriage Act 1949. Although this fact would not have made the marriage void they also knew that the priest was not licensed to conduct the ceremony and that notice of marriage had not been given to the superintendent registrar. The priest had advised the coupe that a civil ceremony should take place but they did not do this so the marriage was void.

Section 11 (b) that at the time of the marriage either party was already married or in a civil partnership. Such a marriage is void.

Section 11(c) that the parties are not respectively male and female. Same sex-marriages are not permitted under English law.

Section 11(d) in the case of a polygamous marriage entered into outside England and Wales, that either party was, at the time, domiciled in England and Wales. Polygamous marriages celebrated abroad have become a common occurrence in England with immigrants returning to their country of origin where polygamous marriages are legal, and marry. However, if either party to the marriage is domiciled in England the marriage will be void.

Voidable marriages

Section 12 of the Matrimonial Causes Act details six grounds that are available for declaring a marriage voidable.

They are:
(a) non-consummation of marriage due to the incapacity of either party
(b) non-consummation of marriage due to the willful refusal of the respondent
(c) lack of valid consent to the marriage by either party
(d) that either party was suffering from mental disorder
(e) that the respondent was suffering from VD in a communicable form at the time of the marriage
(f) that the respondent was pregnant by someone other than the petitioner at the time of marriage.

The grounds most petitioners use for annulment of a voidable marriage are those relating to non-consummation.

Judicial Separation

Although most whose marriage have broken down will get divorced, there are some who, for various reasons will not wish to terminate the marriage, for example for religious reasons. A judicial separation suits such circumstances and although it does not terminate the marriage it will effectively relieve the petitioner of the responsibility of cohabiting with the other party.

Other people may go for judicial separation because they wish to obtain one of the financial orders that a court has the power to make once a separation is granted. The grounds for judicial separation mirror the five facts for divorce. They fall within section 17(1) of the Matrimonial Causes Act.

Forced marriages

The Forced Marriage (Civil Protection) Act 2007 came into force in Autumn 2008. This is an Act that makes provision for protecting individuals from being forced into entering into marriages without their full consent and for protecting individuals who have been forced into marriage without such consent. The Act amends the Family Law Act 1996, Part 4, inserting 4A and provided the courts with powers to make a forced marriage protection order, essentially voiding such marriages. As of 16th June 2014 there are two new criminal offences relating to forced marriage. Section 63CA of the Family Law Act 2016 creates a criminal offence of breaching a forced marriage protection order, which carries a maximum sentenceof five years imprisonment. In addition, s121 Anti Social behaviour and Policing Act makes it a criminal offence to use violence, threats, or any other form of coercion to cause someone to enter into a forced marriage. This offence is punishable by up to seven years imprisonment.

The Marriage (same Sex Couples) Act 2013

The Marriage (Same Sex Couples) Act 2013 came into force on 17 July 2013 and allows same-sex couples the same right to marry as opposite-sex couples.

Ceremonies will be able to take place in any civil venue and religious organisations will have the opportunity to "opt in" to performing religious same-sex marriages. However, the Church of England and the Church in Wales are specifically prevented by the legislation from conducting same-sex marriages.

The new Act remains separate from the Marriage Act 1949, which allows opposite-sex couples to marry, although the provisions are largely the same and afford married same-sex couples the same legal status as married opposite-sex couples. The term "marriage" and "married couple" is now extended to include same-sex couples.

However, there are some differences between the provisions for annulment and divorce for same-sex marriages in the Marriage (Same Sex Couples) Act and those provided for same-sex couples in the Matrimonial Causes Act 1973.

One of the grounds upon which an opposite-sex marriage may be annulled is for non-consummation due to the incapacity of either party to consummate it or the wilful refusal of the other spouse to consummate it. Although a same-sex marriage may also be annulled, the non-consummation ground does not apply.

In obtaining a divorce, an opposite-sex spouse may rely on the adultery of the other to prove that the marriage has irretrievably broken down. The definition of adultery is *"voluntary sexual intercourse between two persons of the opposite sex, of whom one or both is married but who are not married to each other"*. The Marriage (Same Sex Couples) Act has amended the Matrimonial Causes Act to add that *"only conduct between the respondent and a person of the opposite sex may constitute adultery for the purposes of this section."* A same-sex spouse would therefore be unable to obtain a divorce based on adultery (although any alleged infidelity with another person of the same sex could be used as evidence of unreasonable behaviour in support of a divorce application).

The new legislation also makes some alterations to the Gender Reassignment Act 2004, as it will now be possible for a transgender person to remain married after changing their gender, provided their spouse agrees.

Previously, an application for a Gender Recognition Certificate (to be recognised legally as a person of the opposite sex) had to include a statutory declaration as to whether or not the applicant was married or in a civil partnership, as obtaining the Gender Recognition Certificate (GRC) would have the effect of making the marriage or civil partnership void.

Following the new legislation, a married person applying for a GRC may remain married if their spouse consents. Applications for GRCs will now have to include a statutory declaration stating where the marriage took place together with a statutory declaration from the applicant's spouse to say that they consent to the marriage continuing after the issue of a full GRC. If the spouse does not consent, a statutory declaration will need to be made by the applicant to say that their spouse has not made a statutory declaration consenting to the marriage continuing, and the marriage will be made void.

A same-sex marriage remains distinct from a civil partnership, although couples who have previously entered into a civil partnership will be able to convert it into a marriage by way of an application. The resulting marriage will then be treated as having begun on the date of the civil partnership.

Civil partnerships currently remain available only to opposite-sex couples but the Government has indicated that it will review this in the near future. A recent consultation found that 61% of respondents supported civil partnerships being made available to same-sex couples as well as opposite-sex couples. Similar provisions are in force in several European countries including France and The Netherlands, where the majority of couples opting for civil partnerships are opposite-sex.

****

Ch.3

Civil Partnerships

A civil partnership is a legal relationship, which can be registered by two people of the same sex. Same-sex couples, within a civil partnership can obtain legal recognition for their relationship and can obtain the same benefits generally as married couples. Civil Partnerships can now be converted into marriage as a result of the Marriage (Same Sex Couples) Act 2013.

The Civil Partnership Act 2004 came into force on 5th December 2005. The first civil partnerships registered in England and Wales took place on 21st December 2005. Civil partners will be treated the same as married couples in many areas, including:

- Tax, including inheritance tax
- Employment benefits
- Most state and occupational pension benefits
- Income related benefits, tax credits and child support
- Maintenance for partner and children
- Ability to apply for parental responsibility for a civil partners child
- Inheritance of a tenancy agreement
- Recognition under intestacy rules
- Access to fatal accidents compensation
- Protection from domestic violence
- Recognition for immigration and nationality purposes

The registration of a civil partnership

Two people may register a civil partnership provided they are of the same sex, not already in a civil partnership or legally married, not closely related and both over 16 although consent of a parent or guardian must be obtained if either of them are under 18.

Registering a civil partnership is a secular procedure and is carried out by the registration service, which is responsible for the registration of births, deaths and marriages. A civil partnership registration is carried out under what is termed a standard procedure, which can be varied to take into account housebound people or people who are ill and are not expected to recover.

The standard procedure for registering a civil partnership

A couple wishing to register a civil partnership just have to decide the date they want to register and where they want the registration to take place. The formal process for registering consists of two main stages-the giving of a notice of intention to register and then the registration of the civil partnership itself.

The first stage, the giving of notice is a legal requirement and both partners have to do this at a register office in the area of a local authority where they live, even if they intend to register elsewhere. The notice contains the names, age, marital or civil partnership status, address, occupation, nationality and intended venue for the civil partnership. It is a criminal offence to give false information.

If one of the partners is a non-EAA citizen and subject to immigration controls (see later) there are additional requirements to be fulfilled. Once the notice has been given it is displayed at the relevant register office for 15 days. This provided an opportunity for objections to be made. The civil partnership cannot be registered until after 15 clear days have elapsed from the date of the second person gives notice.

Each partner needs to give notice in the area that they have lived for at least seven days. If the couple live in different areas then each will post a notice in their own relevant area. When giving notice they will be asked where they wish the civil partnership to take place.

Residency requirements for a civil partnership

A couple can register a civil partnership in England and Wales as long as they have both lived in a registration district in England and Wales for at least seven days immediately before giving notice. If one person lives in Scotland and the other lives in England or Wales, the person living in Scotland may give notice there. Officers, sailors or marines on board a Royal Navy ship at sea can give notice to the captain or other commanding officer, providing they are going to register with someone who is resident in England and Wales. Service personnel based outside England and Wales have to fulfil the above residence requirements.

Documentary evidence of name, age and nationality will need to be shown. Passports and birth certificates are the main documents required. Proof of address will be required. If either partner has been married or in a civil partnership before evidence of divorce or dissolution will be required. If either partner is subject to immigration control a document showing entry clearance granted to form a civil partnership will need to be shown, along with a home office certificate of approval and indefinite leave to remain in the UK.

Civil partnership registration

A civil partnership registration can take place in any register office in England and Wales or at any venue that has been approved to hold a civil partnership. Approved premises include stately homes and other prestigious buildings including hotels and restaurants. From 5th December 2005, any venue that has approval for civil marriage will automatically be approved for civil partnerships. A civil partnership cannot be registered at a religious premises. A civil partnership can only be registered between the hours of 8am to 6pm unless one person is seriously ill and is not expected to recover.

A civil partnership is legally registered once the couple have signed the legal document, known as a civil partnership schedule, in the

29

presence of a registrar and two witnesses. On the day, two witnesses will be required. If they wish to do so, the couple will be able to speak to each other the words contained in the schedule:

' I declare that I know of no legal reason why we may not register as each other's civil partner. I understand that on signing this document we will be forming a civil partnership with each other'

No religious service may take place, as the process of forming a civil partnership is entirely secular. A ceremony can be arranged to accompany the actual registration. This ceremony can take place at any venue as long as it is approved.

Special circumstances

Variations to the standard procedure can be made in certain circumstances. If a partner is seriously ill and is not expected to recover then a civil partnership can be registered at any time. The 15-day waiting period will not apply. A certificate will need to be provided from a doctor stating that a person is not expected to recover and cannot be moved to a place where civil partnerships take place and that they understand the nature and purpose of signing the Registrar Generals licence.

Housebound people

If one partner is housebound there are special procedures to allow them to register a civil partnership at home. A statement has to be signed, made by a doctor, confirming that this is the case and that the condition is likely to continue for the next three months. The statement must have been made no more than 14 days before notice being given and must be made on a standard form provided by the register office. The normal 15-day period will apply between giving notice and the civil partnership registration.

Detained people

There are special procedures to allow a couple to register a civil partnership at a place where one of them is detained in a hospital or prison. The couple has to provide a statement, made by the prison governor or responsible person confirming that the place where a person is detained can be named in the notice of proposed civil partnership as the place where the registration is to take place. This statement must have been made no more than 21 days prior to notice being given. The normal 15 day waiting period applies.

Family relationships
The law now recognises the role of both civil partners in respect of a child living in their household.

Adoption
Under the Adoption and Children Act 2002, which came into force on 30th December 2005, civil partners may apply jointly to adopt a child.

Parental responsibility
Under the Adoption and Children Act 2002, a person will also be able to acquire parental responsibility for the child of their civil partner. They can do this with the agreement of their civil partner.

If the child's other parent also has parental responsibility, both parents must agree. Parental responsibility can also be acquired on application to the court. Civil partners will have a duty to provide maintenance for each other and any children of the civil partnership.

Dissolution of a civil partnership
A civil partnership ends only on the death of one of the civil partners, or on the dissolution of the partnership or a nullity order or a presumption of death order by the court.

The usual route is for one of the partners to seek a dissolution order to terminate the civil partnership. Other options are available. If one party, for example, did not validly consent as a result of duress, mistake or unsoundness of mind, then a nullity order may be sought from the court. Or if both civil partners do not wish to terminate the partnership one of them may ask the court for a separation order.

The dissolution process

Whoever decides to end the civil partnership should seek legal advice. The case will usually be dealt with by a civil partnership proceedings county court, although complex cases will be referred to the high court.

To end a civil partnership the applicant (petitioner) must prove to the court that the civil partnership has irretrievably broken down. Proof of an irretrievable breakdown is based on the following:

- Unreasonable behaviour by one or other civil partner
- Separation for two years with the consent of the other civil partner
- Separation for five years without the consent of the other civil partner
- If the other civil partner has deserted the applicant for a period of two years or more.

Nullity and voidable partnerships

In exceptional circumstances one party to a civil partnership may decide to seek a court order (a 'Nullity' order) to annul the civil partnership. Section 49 of the CPA 2004 contains the grounds on which the partnership is void, s 50 contains the grounds on which it is voidable and section 51 contains the bars to a decree. The following are grounds (s49) on which a civil partnership may be void:

- The parties are not of the same sex
- Either is already married or in a civil partnership
- Either is under 16
- They are in the prohibited degrees of relationship
- The necessary formalities have not been complied with.

The parties must be of the same sex and there is no provision in relation to polygamous civil partnerships.

Grounds for a civil partnership being voidable

The grounds for a civil partnership being voidable are similar to those for a voidable marriage but are contained within section 50 of the CPA as outlined below. However, it is not possible to annul a civil partnership on the grounds of non-consummation or veneral disease.

Section 50 CPA

- either of them did not validly consent to duress, mistake, unsoundness of mind or otherwise
- either of them, though capable of giving valid consent, was suffering from mental disorder of such a kind or to such an extent as to be unfitted for civil partnership
- at the time of its formation, the respondent was pregnant by some person other than the applicant
- an interim gender recognition certificate has, after the time of its formation, been issued to either civil partner
- the respondent is a person whose gender, at the time of its formation had become the acquired gender under the 2004 Act.

Separation

The grounds on which a separation order may be sought are exactly the same as those for a dissolution order. The end result is different, as a person whose civil partnership has been dissolved is free to marry or form a new partnership whereas a person who has separated remains a civil partner.

Property and financial arrangements

If a civil partnership is ending or if the couple are separating, they will need to decide what happens to any property belonging to them. If they agree on a division they can ask the court to approve the agreement. If they cannot agree they can ask the court to decide. The court has power to make a range of orders in relation to property and other assets including income:

- The court can make an order that one civil partner pay maintenance to the other either for the benefit of the civil partner or for the benefit of any children of the relationship. These orders are known as financial provision orders.
- The court can make an order which will adjust the property rights of the civil partners as regards to property and other assets which they own, either together or separately. This may, for example, mean ordering the transfer and ownership of property from one civil partner to another for that persons benefit or the benefit of any children (known as property adjustment orders)
- The court can make an order in relation to the future pension entitlement of one of the civil partners in favour of the other. This order can relate to occupational pensions, personal pensions and other annuities (known as pension sharing orders)

Financial provision orders for maintenance can be made before a civil partnership has been ended or as separation order granted by the court. Property adjustment and pension sharing orders only take legal effect once dissolution, separation or nullity order has been made by the court.

Even if the couple have been able to agree on maintenance and other property issues they should seek professional advice on such issues. In most cases the solicitor dealing with the end of the civil partnership will be able to provide appropriate advice.

****

Ch.4

When a Relationship Ends

Divorce is the legal process which married couples must go through if they wish to end their marriage formally and revert to a single status.

The United Kingdom has often been referred to as the divorce capital of the world. Whilst that may be an exaggerated claim, in this country 40% of marriages end in divorce, most of them in the age group 25-29. There are many factors attributed to this high rate, not least the increased life span of people and greater economic independence of women. Whatever the explanation, the consequences are severe for society. Children are quite often victims but there are other effects such as increased welfare benefits and stress and depression with the consequent implications for the health system.

The divorce process
The actual procedure for getting divorced is relatively simple. It is an administrative process, rather than a judicial process and is known as the 'special procedure'. Those involved do not normally have to appear in court. One of the spouses, referred to as the petitioner will fill in a set of forms and sign an affidavit confirming the truth of the petition. These will be inspected by a district judge who, if satisfied that all is in order will issue a certificate and a divorce decree will be granted.

Contested petitions
Very few petitions are contested, less than 3%, but if one is contested then there will be a full hearing in front of a judge. A decree of divorce will only be refused when the respondent is able to prove that the petitioners factual statement is incorrect and that the marriage remains viable.

The divorce decree is divided into two parts-the decree nisi, which is the first part and which is announced in open court, usually without the attendance of the parties. The second part, the decree absolute is granted after a period of six weeks has elapsed. Only when the decree absolute is granted can the parties remarry.

Before the court grants the decree, it must be satisfied that arrangements have been made for the welfare of the children under the Matrimonial Causes Act 1973 s 41. If it is not satisfied it will delay the decree absolute.

Divorce-The Ground For Divorce
The Matrimonial Causes Act 1973 governs all matters relating to divorce.

Section 1(1) of the Act states that there is one ground for divorce, that is that the person making an application for a divorce, known as the petitioner, must establish that the marriage has irretrievably broken down. There are two further requirements. First the petitioner must have been married for at least one year and secondly where it is self-evident that the marriage has broken down the petitioner must prove five facts laid down in s 1(2) of the Act:

(a) that the respondent has committed adultery and the petitioner finds it intolerable to live with him/ her. Section 2 (1) of the Matrimonial Causes Act 1973 states that there can be no decree if the parties have lived with each other for more than six months after the discovery of the alleged adultery.

(b) that the respondent has behaved in such a way that the petitioner cannot reasonably be expected to live with him.

When deciding on whether this fact is proved, the court will take into account the characters and personalities of individuals and will attempt objectively to arrive at an interpretation of reasonableness. One significant case was Livingstone-Stallard v Livingstone Stallard (H.C 1974). According to the judge in that case, Dunn j. the question that must be answered is: "Would any right thinking person come to the conclusion that this husband has behaved in such a way that this wife cannot be reasonably expected to live with him, taking into account the whole of the circumstances and the characters and personalities of the parties".

(c) that the respondent has deserted the petitioner for a period of at least two years immediately preceding the presentation of the petition.

A very small percentage of divorce petitions rely on desertion. There are four conditions that must be fulfilled before a spouse will be found to be in desertion:

(a) the parties must be physically living apart
(b) the deserting spouse must have the requisite intention
(c) the separation must not have taken place as a result of an agreement between the parties
(d) the deserting spouse must have had good cause for leaving.
(e) that the parties have lived apart for a continuous period of at least two years immediately preceding the presentation of the petition and the respondent consents to a decree being granted

This fact has two aspects: the period of living apart and the respondents consent. "Living apart" can mean living under the same roof and not living as man and wife, in addition to one party leaving the other. One key case here was Le Brocq v. Le Brocq (1964) where a wife excluded her husband from her bedroom by fixing a bolt on the door. The two parties communicated only when necessary. However she cooked his meals and he paid her weekly housekeeping. It was found that although there was a separation of bedrooms there still existed one household.

d) that the parties have lived apart (agreed separation) for a period of at least two years immediately preceding the presentation of the petition If it can be proven that the separation has lasted at least five years immediately preceding the presentation of the petition then consent of the other side will not be needed to divorce.

There are several key differences between this section. The first is length of time the parties have to have been apart and the fact that the petitioner does not need the other parties consent. However, under section five of the Matrimonial Homes Act the respondent can file a defence that the resulting divorce would mean grave financial or other hardship to him/her and that it would be wrong on these grounds to resolve the marriage. If the court finds that the petitioner can establish another fact for divorce then this undermines the above defence.

The Court will not grant a divorce unless one of the five facts mentioned above has been proved. The court can refuse to grant a decree if it is satisfied that the marriage has not broken down. No petition for divorce can be filed unless the parties have been married for one year.

Judicial separation

Some couples may seek a judicial separation rather than a divorce, although in practice very few do. A judicial separation does not bring a marriage to an end but the court, upon establishing the existenc eof one of the five facts, can grant a separation order. Unlike divorce, a separation order does not remove any benefits that the parties may have under the pension scheme of the other spouse.

people may seek a judicial separation because they have moral or religious objections to divorce, they may not have been married for a year, one of the other bars to divorce might apply or the parties might not be able to prove that the marriage has broken down irretrievably.

Judicial separation does not prevent the parties from obtaining a divorce later. If the parties want to be married again they can request the courts rescind their judicial separation.

****

Ch.5

Rights of Occupation in the Home

Awards of property and financial awards.

The Family Law Act 1996

When homes are vested in one person, complications can arise during or after a divorce. At common law, even though the home (estate) may be vested in the husband, the wife has the right to occupy it. However, this right could be completely undermined by sale of the estate to a third party.

Section 30 of the FLA applies (The Civil Partnerhsips Act 2004 extends this to civil partners) where one spouse (owner) has the right to occupy property that is or was the matrimonial home and the other has not, the other is given 'matrimonial home rights' in that property. There is a right not to be evicted from it without leave of the court and the right to resume occupation if the non-owner is not in occupation (there has been some attempt to evict, for example).

The spouse will only receive benefit of the Act if she needs it. A spouse who already has rights of occupation is not entitled to the statutory rights. Section 30 (9) of the FLA specifically provides that a spouse who only has an equitable interest in the home, and not a legal estate, is to be treated as not being entitled to occupy the house by virtue of that interest. This is of some significance when seeking occupation orders.

The rights exist until termination of the marriage. The rights can also be restricted or terminated by an earlier court order under the FLA s 33 (5).

Creation of rights of occupation between spouses is not the only objective achieved by the FLA. The non-owning spouse must register matrimonial home rights as either a land charge, Class F (for unregistered land), or a notice, for unregistered land. If this is done, then any subsequent purchaser for value will take subject to the statutory rights of occupation. It should be noted, however, that he then has the same rights to apply to the courts for termination or restriction of the matrimonial home rights and his own circumstances, as well as the spouse's, can be taken into account.

The Matrimonial Causes Act 1973 and the Civil Partnerships Act 2004
Under the above orders are made for the benefit of spouses. The court can grant one or more of the following orders for the benefit of a spouse against another:

(a) periodic payments order
(b) a secured periodical payments order
(c) an order for lump sum or sums
(d) a transfer of property order
(e) a settlement of property order
(f) a variation of settlement order
(g) an order extinguishing an interest in a settlement
(h) pension sharing order

None of these orders can be made until a decree of divorce, nullity, dissolution or judicial separation has been granted. Therefore, if the divorce proceedings fail, no order for a spouse can be made under the MCA, ss 23 and 24. All of these orders can be made on the grant of a decree or after. However, a spouse is barred from an order if he or she has remarried prior to the application.

Periodic payments secured and unsecured
This is an order (MCA s23) where one spouse should pay another a periodic sum of money. If it is secured this means that it is charged upon a property owned by the spouse. Secured payments can continue beyond the death of a spouse, unsecured payments do not. The court

has the power to vary or terminate an order. Apart from automatic termination, the court itself has the power to control the duration of both forms of periodical payment. It can order the payments to be made for only a specific length of time and, in addition, can direct that at the end of the specified period the recipient should not be entitled to ask for an extension of the period.

Lump sum

This is an order where one spouse pays another a fixed sum or sums of money. If the lump sum is to be paid in installments then it can be secured on a property.

Transfer of property

This is an order that one spouse transfers to the other property to which the former is entitled. Property can cover anything from houses and flats, jewelry, vehicles, furniture and so on. The M.C.A does not define property. Even if the matrimonial home is mortgaged, it can be the subject of a transfer order, and likewise if it is rented (except for a statutory tenancy under the Rent Act).

Settlement of property order and variation of settlement order

The former is an order that one spouse settle property to which he/she is entitled for the benefit of another. Property is widely interpreted. The variation of a settlement order is an order that any ante- or post-nuptial settlement made on the spouse should be varied for their benefit.

By section 25(1) of the M.C.A. it is provided that, when deciding whether and how to exercise its powers, the court must consider all the circumstances of the case, but give first consideration to the welfare of any minor children of the family. In Suter v. Suter and Jones (C.A. 1986) it was held that giving first consideration to the welfare of the children in financial proceedings did not mean that the welfare of the children overrode all other considerations.

The Child Support Act affects the above, however, where child maintenance is calculated using rigid formula under the jurisdiction of the Child Support Agency, discussed further in chapter 5.

Section 25(2) of the Matrimonial Causes Act directs the court to have regard to the following factors when exercising their powers to make financial provision for a spouse:

a) Income, earning capacity, property and other financial resources. The courts must have regard to the income and capital of both parties, including any that they are likely to have in the foreseeable future. Income includes both earned and unearned income. Capital includes all land, investments, cash and personal possessions. A party's earning capacity is also a resource, including that he is likely to have in the foreseeable future.

One such case in this respect is Leadbeater v Leadbeater (1985) where the wife, aged 47, had been a secretary before marriage but the court thought it unreasonable for her to learn new skills. However, she could have worked longer at her job as a receptionist and her notional earnings were set at £2550, as opposed to her actual income of £1,700.

b) Financial needs, obligations and responsibilities. Again, the court must have regard to all such matters, including those that the parties are likely to have in the foreseeable future. This includes living expenses. Any liabilities of a capital nature are taken into account, such as outstanding mortgage.

(c) Standards of living (enjoyed by family prior to breakdown). In some cases the court will exercise its powers so that the marriage breakdown will have the least possible effect on the standard of living of the parties.

(d) Age of parties and duration of marriage. The age of the parties must be taken into account by the court and can be relevant for a number of reasons. For example, the age of a person may affect promotion prospects or, indeed, whether a job can be found at all.

The duration of the marriage must also be taken into account by the court. There is no definition of what is long or short, but a short marriage is usually taken to mean one of only a few years. Generally, the parties to a short marriage will have less claim on each other than those who have been married for a longer time. However, even a marriage of a shorter duration can produce children, and short marriages between older couples can mean a change in their positions, for example the loss of pension rights previously accrued.

(e) Disabilities. The court must take into account any physical or mental disability of either of the parties to the marriage.

f) Contributions to the welfare of the family. It is specifically provided that this includes any contribution made by looking after the home or caring for the family. Thus the wife, who gives up her job and contributes nothing to the family in hard cash, but is the home-maker and child rearer, has the value of such activities recognised.

g) Conduct. This is a vague principle and relates to gross misconduct, one party against another.

h) The value of any lost benefit. In divorce and nullity cases, the court must take into account the value of any benefit the parties lose the chance of acquiring. This could be, for example, pension rights, which parties might lose on a decree being granted. In Brooks v Brooks, for example, the court compensated the wife by leaving the pension with the husband but giving her other assets. Section 166 of the Pensions Act 1995 enables the court to 'earmark' pensions, that is, to order pension fund managers to pay specific sums to the spouse even where the pension payments are deferred.

In addition to the factors listed above, there are additional considerations for the courts. By section 25A(1) of the M.C.A. the court is placed under a duty to consider whether it is appropriate to make orders that will terminate the parties financial obligations to each other as soon after the decree as it thinks reasonable. Section 25A(2) creates another obligation on the court. If it has decided that an order for periodical payments must be made (thus not ordering a clean break) then it must consider whether to order that the payments must cease after a specified period, a period designed to permit an adjustment to financial independence without undue hardship.

The court has no duty to order a clean break, immediate or delayed; it gives a duty to consider only whether it should order a clean break in every case where it was asked to exercise its financial powers on divorce (or nullity).

Orders for the benefit of children

Children of the family can have the same types of orders made in their favour, against either parties of the marriage, as can the parties themselves.

Financial awards - The Domestic Proceedings and Magistrates Court Act 1978

It may be the case that one party may want an order against another but cannot or does not wish to issue decree proceedings. The D.P.M.C.A. is one of several statutes that gives the courts power to order financial relief without the necessity of first obtaining an order relating to the status of the marriage itself. Three different situations are covered by the Act.

Sections 1 and 2 of the D.P.M.C.A.

Although the applicant is not seeking any type of decree, he still has to establish one of the following grounds set out in section 2:

(a) that the respondent has failed to provide reasonable maintenance for the applicant;

(b) that the respondent has failed to provide or make proper contribution towards the reasonable maintenance of a child of the family;

(c) that the respondent has behaved in such a way that the applicant cannot reasonably be expected to live with him;

(d) that the respondent has deserted the applicant.

There is no definition of the term "reasonable maintenance" in the Act. The court has to take into account the parties respective positions in making their determination. Once the applicant has proved one of the grounds the court has the power to do the following:

(a) make an order that the respondent should pay periodical payments to the applicant and/or a child of the family;

(b) that the respondent should pay a lump sum to the applicant and/or a child of the family, such lump sum not to exceed £1,000.

Orders for periodical payments cease on the death of the payer. Orders for periodical payments to a spouse cease on remarriage of the spouse. The rules for cessation of payments to children are the same as under the Matrimonial Causes Act. Further, orders for periodical payments that are payable to a spouse, either for herself or a child, cease if the parties continue to cohabit or resume cohabitation after the making of the order for a period or periods exceeding six months. Once a ground is proved, a court has to decide whether to make any order at all. Welfare of children is the usual first consideration.

Financial awards - section 27 of the Matrimonial Causes Act 1973

The courts can grant periodical payments, secured or unsecured, and lump sum for spouses and children of the family on proof simply of failure to provide reasonable maintenance. Again, section 27 provides a means of obtaining orders for financial relief without issuing decree proceedings. However, it is another provision that is little used, despite the fact that the range of orders is wider than under the D.P.M.C.A.

Financial and property awards - section 15 of the Children Act 1989

Section 15 of the Children Act provides for the grant of a range of orders for the benefit of a child. The applicant must be a parent of guardian of the child and the orders can be made against a parent.

Orders depend on parenthood not marriage. The nature of the orders possible under the CA is discussed further on in the book.

Unmarried Partners

This section relates to spouses who do not seek a decree and to partners who have never been married to each other. In relation to the former, the following rights are important where divorce is not contemplated, or where a spouse has become insolvent or died. With cohabitees, the Matrimonial Causes Act does not apply. So these are their only rights with regard to joint property. The only difference between the two classes is that cohabitees have to prove to the courts that they had a settled relationship that was intended to be permanent.

Establishing a trust

When dealing with land there will always be documentary evidence as to ownership-the title deeds. It may be that both parties own the land or just one. However, in some case of joint ownership this is not spelt out. Here there is a rebuttable presumption that the legal owners are each entitled to an equal share of the beneficial estate. Further, the legal estate in the home may be vested in the sole name of one of the cohabitees. Here, there is a rebuttable presumption that the beneficial interest also belongs exclusively to that person.

In both these situations consideration of the title deeds alone will not necessarily provide the answer to an ownership dispute. Extrinsic evidence to rebut the presumptions can be adduced, evidence of the existence of a trust behind the deeds. Trusts are generally categorised as express, implied, resulting and constructive. Express trusts are not common in the family context. The other trusts, or distinctions are of little relevance. What is of relevance is the circumstances in which the court will accept that the trust has arisen, whether resulting, implied or constructive.

Payment towards the purchase price

Where one party provides the whole or the part of the purchase price for property that is conveyed into another persons name, there is a rebuttable presumption that the first party intended that he should benefit and the second party should hold the property on trust for him, either exclusively or in part, i.e. the beneficial estate "results" in whole or in part, to A. The trust is therefore known as a resulting trust. The concept of resulting trust is rarely directly applicable in the family context because usually the home is not purchased outright but by way of mortgage.

Two cases in the House of Lords Petit v. Petit (1969) and Gissing V.Gissing (1979) serve to highlight the complicated area of trusts. Both cases concerned a spouse who did not have an interest in the legal estate in the home claiming to be entitled to a beneficial interest by way of trust. There was a unanimous decision in both cases that a trust could arise where both parties had intended that it should. The court should look for a common intention that both parties should be beneficially entitled (common intent). Proof of conduct from which the court can infer the common intent is not sufficient. The woman (in these cases) must also prove that she has acted "to her detriment or significantly altered her position in reliance on the common intent" before a trust in her favour will arise. Therefore, before such a trust can be established, the courts will scrutinise the parties conduct for two reasons: the first to ascertain that there was the common intent; the second to ascertain that the woman has acted upon it. The crucial questions are then seen to be what sort of conduct will give rise to the inference of common intent and what sort of conduct will show that the woman has acted upon it?

The most recent and authoritative statements on these issues are to be found in the leading judgment of Lord Bridge in Lloyds Bank PLC v. Rosset. Express discussions between the parties as to their interests in the property do not amount to conduct from which a common intent can be inferred. What is looked for are:

" direct contributions to the purchase price by the partner who is not the legal owner, whether initially or by payment of mortgage installments". These "will readily justify the inference necessary to the creation of a constructive trust. But...it is extremely doubtful whether anything less will do".

An express agreement
Where there is evidence of the parties having entered into

"an agreement, arrangement or understanding that the property is to be shared beneficially" then, in some circumstances, the court will hold that a trust has arisen. The finding of such an agreement can only be based upon express discussions between the parties.

However, proving an agreement is not the end of the matter. The woman has to show, as before, that she has acted to her detriment or significantly altered her position in reliance on the agreement before the court will hold that a trust in her favour has arisen. Two points need to be made in relation to this type of trust. First, it can be distinguished from an express trust, which does not require an agreement between the parties, nor the woman having acted to her detriment. Second, it can be distinguished from a trust arising from the common intention of the parties, because the court does not infer an agreement. Direct evidence of it must be present.

Again, the crucial issue is the sort of conduct that will be required before, for this type of trust, the woman will be held to have acted to her detriment.

Quantification of beneficial interests under a trust
In the past few years, there have been a number of cases concerning the quantification of shares. Where the cases concern a resulting trust, the shares are determined in relation to each party's contribution. Where the case concerns a trust arising from an express agreement of the parties or a trust arising from their common intent, as inferred from their conduct, the shares are determined by reference to that agreement or, if there is none, their common intent. Where there is no common agreement, the court is entitled to look at:
"all the circumstances surrounding the acquisition of the property, things said and done then and subsequently" including "their respective financial contributions to the purchase price. (B v B H.C. 1988). "the contributions which in total each had made. Those contributions would include, in addition to the original contribution, sums contributed to discharge of the ... mortgage and the cost of capital improvements." (Passee v. Passee (C.A. 1988).

Proprietary Estoppel

Estoppel is the principle that prevents a person from exercising or asserting his legal rights and usually the principle can only be pleaded in defence of an action to exercise or assert those rights. Proprietary estoppel, however, can only be used to assert contrary rights. The circumstances in which such a situation will be recognised by law are rigorously defined. In Coombes v. Smith (H.C. 1987) the court stated that a claim to a share in the beneficial interest of a property based upon proprietary estoppel would only succeed if the claimant can show:

(a) that she had made a mistake as to her legal rights in the property
(b) that she had spent money or done some other legal act as a result of that mistake
(c) that the defendant knew of his own rights in the property inconsistent with those she had
(d) that he knew of her mistaken belief
(e) that he encouraged her to act as above.

Occupation of the home

If a woman is successful in establishing that she has a beneficial interest in the property, she may then be faced with a demand that nevertheless the property be sold so that the man may at least realise his share. This could equally happen to a woman who is a joint owner on the face of the deeds. An immediate sale of the home can cause hardship.

By the Law of Property Act 1925 s30 the court can order the sale of the property subject to a trust for sale. But it can also refuse to make such an order. Generally it will do so if it is satisfied that the purpose of the trust is still unfulfilled. Thus if the home was in reality bought as a home for the family, it is likely that any application for the sale of the home prior to the children reaching majority age will be refused, despite the breakdown of marriage. Thus there is protection for the woman here, to some extent.

49

Because of the facts of their relationship the woman may not be able to establish that they own a share of the property. As a last resort, such a woman may be at least able to establish a right to occupy a home after the relationship has broken down.

This may be possible if the circumstances show that he has granted her a licence to stay on his property, a licence that was given for consideration and cannot be revoked by giving notice but only in accordance with the contract.

Courts are often asked to infer the granting of such licences. In Tanner v. Tanner (C.A. 1975) because the woman gave up a protected tenancy to go and live with the man and their children at his house, the court inferred the grant of a licence to occupy until his children left school. However, in Coombes v. Smith the court rejected the alternative claim of the plaintiff for a licence for the duration of her life.

The inference of a licence of this kind is based on the facts of each case and can be an extremely artificial exercise.

****

Ch.6

Provision for Children-The Current System of Child Maintenance

The Child Support Agency, was brought into being by the Child Support Act 1991. The purpose of the agency was to improve on the then existing child maintenance system that, according to the government allowed errant fathers to avoid maintenance with no real sanctions. The Government stated:

"The present system is unnecessarily fragmented, uncertain in its results, slow and ineffective. It is largely based on discretion. The cumulative effect is uncertainty and inconsistent decisions about how much maintenance should be paid".

The C.S.A eventually came into force on April 5th 1993. The agency was responsible for all new cases, cases where the claimant is on income support and family credit. In 1995, in response to further criticism, the government introduced further legislation in the 1995 Child Support Act, which in turn has been amended by the Child Support, Pensions and Social Security Act 2000. This in turn was amended by the Child Maintenance and Other Payments Act 2008 which produced further changes to the rules governing child maintenance. This Act introduced key changes as follows:

- There was no obligation for people on benefits to use the Child Maintenance and Enforcement Commission
- The Child Support Agency no longer exists and was subsumed by the CMEC

- The Commission was under the power of the Secretary of State for Work and Pensions
- The main object of the Commission was to 'maximise the number of those children who live apart from one or both of their parents for whom effective maintenance arrangements are in place'.

The Commissions main objective was supported by the following subsidiary objectives:

a) To encourage and support the making and keeping by parents of appropriate voluntary maintenance arrangements for their children,
b) To support the making of applications for child support maintenance under the Child Support Act 1991 and to secure compliance when appropriate with parental obligations under that Act,

From Monday 10th December 2012 a new system of child maintenance began operation, initially for specific applicants. It is known as the 'Child Maintenance Service', and operates within the legislation provided under the Welfare Reform Act 2012 and is under the auspices of the Department of Work and Pensions. Existing cases continue under previous legislation at present. Below is an outline of the powers of the CSA

What is child maintenance?
Child maintenance is regular, reliable financial support that helps towards the child's everyday living costs. The parent who does not have main day-to-day care of the child (the non-resident parent) pays child maintenance to the parent who does have main day-to-day care (the parent with care). In some cases, this person can be a grandparent or guardian.

In addition to regular child maintenance payments, parents can also choose to make payments 'in kind'. This is where the parent without the main day-to-day care pays for things directly, such as clothing, bills or school costs.

The parent with day-to-day care of the child as the "parent with care" and the parent without day-to-day care as the "non-resident parent."

Child maintenance arrangements

A family-based arrangement
Parents with the main day-to-day care of a child, regardless of whether they are benefit claimants, can choose to come to a family-based arrangement with the other parent. Both parents agree on a regular amount to be paid, which can include payments in kind, where one parent pays for things like taking their child on holiday, buying clothes or food – essentially whatever they decide suits their family circumstances.

A statutory arrangement

The statutory maintenance service, currently operated by the Child Support Agency (CSA), helps put in place a statutory arrangement, supporting parents when a family-based arrangement is not appropriate, or breaks down. The CSA takes responsibility for putting the arrangement in place and maintaining it. The CSA can use a range of enforcement powers to take action against those parents who fail to fulfil their responsibilities to pay. The CSA provides two types of service: assessment and collection where the CSA calculates liability and collects payments; and assessment only where the CSA calculates liability but payments are arranged and made directly between the parents (Maintenance Direct). Maintenance Direct can be agreed by both parent with care and non-resident parent on initial set up or at any time during the life cycle of the case.

Through the Courts

Parents in England and Wales who decide to establish a family-based arrangement can register it as a consent order with the Courts. If parents choose to have a consent order, they can later apply to the statutory maintenance service but only after the order has been in place for at least 12 months. Parents in Scotland have similar arrangements where a family-based arrangement can be registered to make it a legally binding 'Minute of Agreement'. They can later apply to the statutory maintenance service but only after the agreement has been in place for at least 12 months. For further details about setting up a child maintenance arrangement visit Child Maintenance Options at www.cmoptions.org

What is Child Maintenance Options?

Child Maintenance Options is a national service which provides impartial information and support to enable parents to make an informed choice about which of the different types of child maintenance arrangement is most appropriate for them.

The service was developed with significant input from voluntary and community sector organisations as well as other key partners. The service is delivered by phone, via a website and for those in most need of more personalised help, through a face-to-face service. It is available for use by separating and separated parents, as well as family, friends, grandparents, guardians, and anyone else with an interest in child maintenance.

Child Maintenance Options can also provide practical support on many of the other issues that parents may face when parenting apart, for example, housing and employment. Child Maintenance Options is the first port of call for anyone with a query about child maintenance. Alternatively, they can be contacted via the website at www.cmoptions.org 0800 988 0988

The CSA

Child maintenance schemes through the CSA will be phased out between now and 2017 and claimants will be encouraged to contact Child maintenance options. Until that time, the CSA contiunes to operate two statutory schemes of child maintenance. These are:

- The 1993 scheme (often referred to as the old scheme, for clients whose applications were made between 1993 and March 2003).This scheme is no longer open for new applications.
- The 2003 scheme (often referred to as the current scheme, for applications made after March 2003)

How does the CSA work out how much child maintenance should be paid?

The 1993 scheme and the 2003 scheme have different means of calculating how much maintenance is payable. The 1993 scheme formula (old scheme) was more complicated and required a large amount of information. The amount of maintenance payable depended on the circumstances and income of both the parent with care and the non-resident parent. Although no applications can now be made to the old scheme, the amount of maintenance which clients on this scheme pay is still calculated using this formula.

The 2003 scheme (current scheme) is worked out by applying one of four rates to the non-resident parent's 'net weekly income'. Income is defined as earnings, money from an occupational or personal pension and in certain circumstances tax credits. The four rates applied to the non-resident parent's income are:

- Basic rate (if they have an income of £200 a week or more);
- Reduced rate (if their income is more than £100 but less than £200 a week);
- Flat rate (if their income is £5 to £100 a week or they are on prescribed benefits), and

- Nil rate (if their income is less than £5 a week or they are in a prescribed category e.g. prisoners).
- Other factors can also affect the amount payable. The CSA can adjust the child maintenance calculation based on:
- The number of other children living with the non-resident parent, for whom they or their partner get child benefit;
- The number of children the non-resident parent needs to pay child maintenance for, and Whether the child stays with the non-resident parent at least one night a week.

What information does the CSA need to work out child maintenance?

To help the CSA work out how much child maintenance should be paid, it will normally ask for some basic information from both parents. It will need to know:

- Full addresses and phone numbers for both parents;
- The non-resident parent's income;
- The number of children for whom child maintenance should be paid; and
- The number of other children who live with the non-resident parent.

Either parent can apply to the CSA to put a maintenance arrangement in place, although in most cases, it is the parent with care who makes the application. If the parent with care can give the CSA details of where it can contact the non-resident parent, the CSA will ask non-resident parent for information within four weeks of getting the application. When the CSA has all the information it needs, it will work out child maintenance as soon as possible, usually within 12 weeks.

Enforcement of non-payment

If a non-resident parent falls behind on his/her payments, and an appropriate repayment arrangement cannot be put in place, the CSA has a range of tools which it can use to secure payment.

If the non-resident parent is employed, then the first enforcement step the CSA usually takes is to serve a deduction from earnings order on the non-resident parent's employer to allow the CSA to deduct maintenance directly from the non-resident parent's salary.

If the non-resident parent is not employed, or if the deduction from earnings order is ineffective at recovering the arrears within an appropriate timescale, the CSA will seek to obtain a liability order. This is a legal recognition of an amount of debt accrued over a specified period. The CSA can then take further steps and these vary across the two jurisdictions – England & Wales and Scotland. These include:

- The use of bailiffs to seize assets (in England & Wales) or the attachment of assets by Sheriff Officers for sale at auction (in Scotland);
- An order to put up for sale the non-resident parent's residential property (in England & Wales) or the registration of an Inhibition which prevents the non-resident parent transferring or disposing of heritable property and may affect the parent's ability to obtain credit, loans or mortgages (in Scotland);
- Driving licence disqualification;
- Deduction of maintenance payments and/or arrears from the non-resident parent's bank account;
- A Freezing Order, preventing the parent from selling or transferring ownership of an asset,
- Recovering arrears from a deceased parent's estate; and
- Imprisonment.

Child maintenance arrangements and benefit claims?

Previously, parents on benefits with the main day-to-day care of their child were compelled to use the statutory maintenance service, and were only able to keep up to £10 of the child maintenance paid depending on the scheme rules before it affected their benefits.

From October 2008, this child maintenance disregard was increased to £20 per week. Child maintenance was also fully disregarded when calculating Housing Benefit and Council Tax Benefit claims.

On 12 April 2010, a full maintenance disregard was introduced, which means for parents with the main day-to-day care of the child(ren) any maintenance received is no longer taken in account when calculating their benefit entitlement.

Tax credits – why this is considered income when calculating maintenance?
The inclusion of tax credits is defined in child support legislation under Schedule 1 Part IV of the Child Support (Maintenance Calculations and Special Cases) Regulations 2000, which can be accessed online at: http://www.dwp.gov.uk/docs/o-8701.pdf

Both working and child tax credits are treated as a non-resident parent's income as they are paid as a supplement to earnings. In circumstances where the non-resident parent and their partner are working, half of the working tax credits received will be included within the non-resident parent's net weekly income in order to calculate his or her liability. If the non-resident parent's partner receives the household primary income, no tax credits will be included as part of the income figure for the purposes of the maintenance calculation. Child tax credits paid to either the non-resident parent or their partner is taken into account in full.

The reason for the inclusion of tax credits within the maintenance calculation is that if earnings rise, receipt of tax credits reduces accordingly. It therefore seems consistent and fair that the tax credit entitlement, which is a sum derived from earnings, should be included within a non-resident parent's income for the calculation of child maintenance.

What age does a child have to be for the parent with care to be eligible to receive child maintenance?

A "qualifying child" is currently defined in child support legislation as;

- Under the age of 16;
- Between 16 and 19, and undertaking full-time, non-advanced education;
- Between 16 and 19, and registered with certain types of government-approved training courses and child benefit is in payment.

The child also must be habitually resident in the UK and living in the same residence as the parent/person with care, although there are some exceptions to this rule, for example children who are at boarding school or have long term hospitalisation are still classed as qualifying children.

Can the CSA collect child maintenance payments when a qualifying child, parent with care or non-resident parent live outside the UK?

The CSA has no legal authority to act where one or more of the non resident parent, the parent with care or the child lives abroad, but the courts may be able to take action. It is a requirement of the legislation that all parties subject to a CSA maintenance calculation must be 'habitually resident' within the UK. However the CSA may have jurisdiction in some exceptional circumstances, which include if the non-resident parent:

- Is working abroad in the service of the Crown, for example is a civil servant or works within Her Majesty's diplomatic service or within Her Majesty's Overseas Civil Service;
- Is a member of the UK Armed Forces;
- Works abroad for a UK based company, for example if the company employs people to work outside the UK but makes payments via a UK payroll; and the company is registered under the Companies Act

1985 (England, Wales and Scotland) or the Companies (Northern Ireland) Order 1986; or

• Works abroad on secondment for a prescribed body, for example for an NHS trust, regional health authority, primary care trust or local authority.

If the non-resident parent lives abroad and does not fall into one of the categories above then the parent with care can apply to the courts for child maintenance. The UK has arrangements with more than 100 countries and territories that allow a person living in one jurisdiction to claim maintenance from an ex-partner living in another via the courts.

What happens if the non-resident parent lives abroad?

If the non-resident parent lives in the European Union and the parent with care lives in the UK, decisions made by the CSA can be enforced in other member states.

From 18 June 2011, there has been a legal requirement within the European Union for member states to enforce maintenance orders made by courts or by the CSA within member states. However member states can only enforce arrears built up on CSA cases when both parents were resident in the UK.

The parent with care can make an application to the Reciprocal Enforcement of Maintenance Orders (REMO) unit at the Office of the Official Solicitor and Public Trustee if the non-resident parent lives in the European Union. If the non-resident parent does not live in the European Union then the parent with care can apply to the UK courts for child maintenance.

Maintenance orders made by UK courts on behalf of UK residents can be registered and enforced by courts or other authorities in other countries against people who live there. Parent with care can also ask foreign authorities to create an order for maintenance on their behalf. A UK resident who wishes to apply to obtain maintenance from a person overseas should approach their local magistrates' court (or county court where the order was made) if they have an existing court order for maintenance or their local magistrates' court (or sheriff court in Scotland) if there is no existing order

The UK authorities have no power to compel foreign courts or authorities to enforce maintenance orders, or to set a timescale for enforcement, as the system is based on mutual agreement. Every effort is made, however, to encourage foreign agencies to abide by their countries' international obligations.

Parents with care do not have to engage a solicitor. Court staff will help and will forward the application to the relevant authority in the UK. The UK authority will check that the application is in order and send it to the foreign authority or court for registration and enforcement against the person living there.

Disputes about the parentage of a child

There are a number of methods by which the CSA can resolve parentage disputes.

Presumed parentage

Child support legislation provides:

A named person can be presumed to be the father of a child, where the child has not subsequently been legally adopted if:

- They were married to the mother at any time between the date the child was conceived and the date the child was born.
- They are named as the father of the child on the birth certificate.

A named person may be presumed to be the parent of a child if:

- They refuse to take a DNA test;
- They have taken a DNA test and there is no reason to doubt they are the parent;
- They have adopted the child;

- They are named in a court order as a parent;
- They may by law be presumed the parent of a child born as a result of fertility treatment.

If a person wishes to appeal on the grounds they are not the parent of the child they must provide evidence that this is the case. If the person provides conclusive evidence that they are not the parent of a child, the CSA will refund all child maintenance payments made from the date that their evidence was received. Conclusive evidence is considered to be DNA test results from an approved list of DNA suppliers or a 'declaration of non-parentage' from a court.

How is a non-resident parent's child maintenance liability affected when both parents share the care of their child or children?

Where the CSA works out how much maintenance the non-resident parent should pay, a reduction can apply where the parents share the care of the child. This reduction may only apply where care is shared overnight. Where the reduction for "shared care" is applied, the amount of maintenance payable is reduced pro-rata by the number of nights a week the child stays with the non-resident parent.

Under the 1993 child maintenance scheme the non-resident parent must provide at least 104 nights of care per year in order to qualify for the shared care reduction. In the 2003 child maintenance scheme, the non-resident parent must provide at least 52 nights of care per year. Separate provisions, based on a similar principle, are applicable when the care of a child or children is shared equally between both parents.

What happens if the child spends an equal amount of time with both parents?

In 2003 scheme cases, if the care of a child is shared equally between both parents (that is they spend 175 nights with both parents) the CSA:

- divide the weekly amount of child maintenance by two, and reduce the amount of child maintenance again by another £7 a week for each child. The amount of £7 is set down in law.

In these situations parents are encouraged to come to their own financial arrangement in addition to the calculation.

In 1993 scheme cases the child must spend an average of two nights a week (usually averaged over the last 12 months) with the non-resident parent before the amount of child maintenance will be reduced.

What decisions made by the CSA can people appeal against?

Each time the CSA makes a decision about the amount of child maintenance that a non-resident parent must pay, either parent has the right to appeal against it. There are other decisions they can appeal against.

What should parents do if they are not happy about the service provided by the CSA?

In the first instance they should contact the people dealing with their case, either by phone or in writing. They can find contact details on letters. They can also e-mail their complaint to us by using the online complaints forms. If the people dealing with the case cannot settle the complaint they will send it to the CSA's Complaints Resolution Team. If a parent is not happy with the response from the Complaints Resolution Team they can ask for their complaint to be considered by the Complaints Review Team.

Allowance given for relevant other children

The Department has a legislative responsibility to consider the welfare of all children connected to a maintenance case including, but not limited to, decisions on the appropriate maintenance assessment and about enforcement action to recover arrears. This requirement to consider the welfare of any child as set out in the Child Support Act 1991, Schedule 1, paragraph 10C (2) (a) is not limited solely to the biological children of the parents involved.

The reason for the allowance within the maintenance calculation is that no parent should be forced to choose between supporting the children they live with now, and those of a previous relationship. Ignoring the needs of children parents live with now in the maintenance calculation could lead to genuine hardship. The policy in this area is specifically designed to take account of all children for whom a parent has financial responsibility, rather than only those to whom the parent is biologically related.

The absent parent now has a new partner and children to support

The principle underpinning the statutory child maintenance service is that a parent's responsibility to support his or her child is an obligation which should have the highest priority and that this financial responsibility is absolute. Child maintenance is a contribution towards the cost of bringing up a child and this includes not only such items as food and clothing but also it is a contribution towards the home that the child lives in and the associated costs of running that home.

Under the 2003 child maintenance scheme the income of the parent with care or their partner is not relevant to the child maintenance calculation and does not affect the non-resident parent's liability to contribute to the support of their child or children. The child maintenance calculation is based entirely on the net income of a non-resident parent and is an approximation of what they would spend if their child lived with them. Allowances are applicable if the non-resident has other children living within their household.

The statutory child maintenance service does not guarantee a particular financial outcome for a child within the service; it ensures parents take a degree of financial responsibility for their children. What the parent with care is receiving should not remove the responsibility of a non-resident parent to support their child and in most cases the parent with care will be supporting the child through the provision of a home and related expenses. This is why the majority of non-resident parents, including those with lower incomes or who are receiving benefits, are required to make at least some contribution to the support of their child.

Matrimonial Causes Act 1973, as amended by the Matrimonial and Family Proceeding Act 1984.

Within the framework of the above children can have the same types of orders made in their favour, against either of the parties to the marriage as can the parties themselves. The order can direct payment to the child or third party. Generally, no application for an order in favour of a child over 18 can be made. Periodical payments orders secured or unsecured must terminate when the child reaches 17 unless the court decides to the contrary. Both types of payments must cease on the death of the payer.

Matters taken into account when making an order

As with spouse orders, the first consideration of the court, when deciding whether and how to exercise it powers, is the welfare of any minor children of the family. The courts, under M.C.A. s 25(3) will have regard to:

a) the financial needs of the child
b) the income, earning capacity, property and other financial resources of the child
c) any physical or mental disability of the child
d) the type of education or training he was receiving or was expected to receive by the parties to the marriage
e) the financial assets and needs of the parties, the standard of living enjoyed by the family prior to the breakdown of the marriage and any physical or mental disability of the parties.

The M.C.A. s 25(4) provides further factors to be taken into account when the court is considering making an order against a party to the marriage who is not a parent of the child, and include, for example the liability of any other person to maintain the child.

The Children Act 1989, Section 15

Section 15 of the CA provides for the grant of a range of financial and property awards for children subject to the C.S.A. The applicant must be the parent or guardian of the child and orders can be made against the parent.

It must be remembered that the availability of these orders is not dependent upon the parties being married to each other, it is dependent upon parenthood. However, married parents may make use of section 15 where there is no pending divorce proceedings.

The court has the power to make the following orders:

a) that either parent pay periodical payments for the benefit of the child, secured or unsecured

b) that either parent pay a lump sum for the benefit of the child

c) that either parent transfer property to which he is entitled to the child

d) that either parent do settle such property for the benefit of the child.

Payments and transfer for the benefit of the child can be ordered to be made direct to the child or to some third party. It should be noted that if applications are made to magistrates courts, the only orders that can be made are ones for unsecured periodical payments and lump sums not exceeding £1,000. All the above orders benefit children alone. Orders for unsecured periodical payments cease on the death of the payer and for both types of periodical payments the rules for cessation when the child reaches a specific age apply.

The CA schedule one lists the matters that the court must take into account when deciding what order to make. They bear some similarity to those listed in the M.C.A. s 25(3), the factors relevant for child orders ancillary to decree proceedings.

Ch.7

Domestic Violence

Definition of domestic violence
As from March 2013 the Government's definition of domestic violence and abuse is extended to include people aged 16 and 17. the definition is:

Any incident or pattern of incidents of controlling, coercive or threatening behaviour, violence or abuse between those aged 16 or over who are or who have been intimate partners or family members regardless of gender or sexuality. This can encompass, but is not limited to, the following types of abuse:

- psychological
- physical
- sexual
- financial
- emotional

The Governemnt's definition goes on to explain:
- controlling behaviour is a range of acts designed to make a person subordinate and/or dependent by isolating them from sources of support, exploiting their resources and capacities for personal gain, depriving them of the means of independence, resistance and escape and regulating their everyday behaviour. Coercive behaviour is an act or pattern of acts or assault, threats, humiliation and intimidation or other abuse that is used to harm, punish or frighten their victims.

The definition also includes 'honour' based violence, femal genital mutilation and forced marriage. Domestic villence can also include violence between parents and children and other areas such as psychological games and breaking of trust, plus financial control.

The Family Law Act 1996

Harm is defined in s63(1) Family law Act 1996:

    i)   in relation to an adult: ill treatment or the impairment of health

    ii)   for a child: ill treatment or impairment of health or development (physical, social, emotional or educational;

    iii)

    iv)   includes sexual abuse and forms of ill treatment which are not physical.

The Adoption and Children Act 2002 adds into that definition harm caused by 'seeing or hearing violence perpetrated upon another' a recognition of the emotional harm caused to children who witness domestic violence.

Violence in the family is a common occurrence and can cause a great deal of misery to the victim of that violence. Although violence is not just physical but mental too, it is an unfortunate fact that much of the incidence of domestic violence is by men against women. Physical violence is a criminal offence. However, the criminal law is concerned primarily with punishment and does not take any steps to protect the victim. This section is concerned with civil remedies, mainly the injunction. An injunction can be granted to restrain violence and also molestation.

Horner v. Horner (1983) defined molestation as "any conduct which can properly be regarded a such a degree of harassment as to call for the intervention of the court". There are cases where an injunction restraining such behaviour will not be sufficient protection. In these case there can be no real alternative but to make an order separating the parties, an order which ousts one of them from the home.

These orders, ouster orders have many variations, for example, to prevent one party using certain rooms in the house or an ouster from the house or even the area.

Most commonly the woman seeks an order against the man. The powers can equally be used by man against woman.

Inherent Jurisdiction

By section 37(1) of the Supreme Courts Act 1981, the High Court is given the power to grant injunctions "in all cases in which it appears to be just and convenient to do so". This power is also given to the county court by section 38 of the County Courts Act 1984.

In the family law sphere, this power is frequently used to grant non-molestation injunctions as a part of a divorce suit. An injunction under these Acts can only be granted in support of a legal or equitable right. It is accepted that everyone has a right not to be subjected to assault and battery and this has been relied upon by the courts, expressly or impliedly, when granting a wife a non-molestation injunction against her violent husband, as part of divorce proceedings. It is possible, however, that such injunctions are too wide.

In the case Patel v. Patel (1988) an injunction restraining the respondent from "assaulting, molesting or otherwise interfering or communicating with the applicant" had been granted to an unmarried woman as part of an action alleging trespass to the person. It was redrawn by the court to restrain, assault and molestation only. This was ordered on the basis that there is no right not to be harassed that could be supported by the words "otherwise interfering or communicating with".

Ouster injunctions present a different problem. Since Richards v. Richards, applications for ouster orders between spouses have to be made under the Matrimonial Homes Act. In practice, they may still be dealt with as part of the divorce proceedings but the Court must apply the principles of the M.H.A. in arriving at their decision. There have been conflicting decisions in the court of appeal concerning the power to grant ouster orders in proceedings concerning children.

In Ashbury v. Millington (1986) the court said it had no powers under the guardianship of Minors Act 1971, nor was there the power under the inherent jurisdiction. This was affirmed by F (minors) (Parental Home: Ouster) (1993) where a mother argued that her father should be excluded from the house so that she could live there with the children. She relied on the inherent jurisdiction and in the alternative, a CA, section 8 specific issue order. Her appeal was dismissed. An injunction under the inherent jurisdiction was not available and section 8 orders could not affect the fathers right of occupation. Finally, the injunction must bear a sensible relationship to the proceedings in which it is sought.

The Family Law Act 1996 Part 1V

Part 1V was implemented on October 1, 1997 and repealed a number of provisions in former Acts, notably the Matrimonial Homes Act 1983 and the Domestic Violence and Matrimonial Proceedings Act 1976. The Law Commission made several proposals in order to bring together all of the former provisions, which were considered highly unsatisfactory, and these are now codified in part 1V.

Associated persons or relevant child

In determining whether a client will be able to obtain a non molestation order under the Family Law Act 1996 the first matter to be ascertained is whether the applicant and respondent are "associated" within the meaning of the Act or, where the person sought to be protected is a child, whether the child is a "relevant "child.

The list of associated persons appears in s. 62 (4) and (5) of the Act and covers persons who, prior to the 1996 Act could not obtain injunctive relief unless they were able to rely upon behaviour which was capable of amounting to a tort or threatened tort and so bring a civil action to which injunctive relief might attach.

Persons are associated with each other if:

(a) they are married;
(b) they have been married;
(c) they are cohabitants;
(d) they are former cohabitants;
(e) they live in the same household;
(f) they have lived in the same household;
(g) they are relatives;
(h) they have agreed to marry each other;
(I) they are parents of the same child;
(j) they have, or have had, parental responsibility for the same child;
(k) they are parties to the same family proceedings.

The exception to this is where one of the parties is a body corporate (local authority).

Not only may they make their own application but they may include in the order a 'relevant child', that is:
-any child who is living with, or might reasonably be expected to live with either of the parents;
-any child in relation to whom an order under the Adoption Act 1976 or the C.A. is in question in the proceedings;
-any other child whose interests the court considers relevant.

Children under 16 can apply for an order with leave and if of sufficient understanding. Under C.A. amendments a parent may be removed from the home instead of taking a child into local authority care.

Non-Molestation Orders
Section 42 of the F.L.A. allows the court to make orders prohibiting a person from molesting a person with whom he is associated and from molesting a relevant child. The order may refer to molestation in general or particular acts of molestation or both, and may be made for

a specified period or until further order. In exercising its discretion the court shall have regard to all the circumstances including the need to secure the health, safety and well being of the applicant or of any relevant child. There is no definition of molestation in the F.L.A. so all existing case law remains relevant.

Domestic Violence Protection Notices and Orders (DVPN) (DVPO)
Sections 24-33 of the Crime and Security Act 2010 provide for the police to issue DVPN's and to apply to the courts for a DVPO. The DVPN can act as an immeditae non-molestation and occupation order, breach of which is an offence. If the police obtain a DVPO, this can contain similar provisons and last for between 14 and 28 days, which is intended to be enough time for the victim to apply for their own non-molestation and occupation orders.

Occupation orders
The Family Law Act attempts to simplify matters by granting courts the power to make a single order in relation to the home. The order is known as an occupation order. They replace ouster orders and are available to 'associated persons'.

There is a distinction drawn, in Section 33 of the F.L.A. between what are known as "non-entitled applicants and "entitled" applicants. Entitled applicants have a legal or beneficial interest in the home, non-entitled applicants do not. Non-entitled applicants can only apply for orders against former spouses, cohabitants or former cohabitants.

An order under Section 33 may:
-enforce the applicants entitlement to enter and or remain in occupation of the house or even part of it;
-prohibit, suspend or restrict the exercise by the respondent of any right of his to occupy the home, including his matrimonial home rights;
-regulate the occupation of the dwelling house by either or both parties.

The courts powers

In deciding whether, and if so, how to exercise its powers the court must have regard to all the circumstances of the case, including:

-the housing needs and housing resources of the parties and of any relevant child:

-the financial resources of any of the parties;

-the likely effect of any order, or of a decision not to make an order, on the health, safety and well being of either party or relevant child or;

-the conduct of the parties in relation to each other or otherwise.

The balance of harm test

The court has complete discretion to make an order except under section 33(7) of the FLA. If it appears to the court that the applicant or any relevant child is likely to suffer any significant harm, attributable to conduct of the respondent if an order is not made, the court shall make the order unless it appears to it that the respondent or any relevant child is likely to suffer significant harm if the order is made, and that harm is as great or greater than the harm which is likely to be suffered by the applicant or child if the order is not made.

Applicant is a former spouse, a cohabitant or a former cohabitant with no existing right to occupy

Section 35 of the FLA applies if a former spouse is entitled to occupy a dwelling by virtue of a beneficial estate, etc, and the other former spouse is not so entitled: and the house was at any time their matrimonial home or was at any time intended by them to be their matrimonial home. For the purposes of this section, a person claiming an equitable interest in the home is deemed not to have a right to occupy.

Sections 36 and 37 of the Act make similar provisions for cohabitants and ex cohabitants who also do not have rights to occupy the former family home. Where the applicant is a former spouse, the court shall have regard not only to the matters set out in section 33\96\0 but also:

-the length of time that has elapsed since the parties ceased to live together;
-the length of time that has elapsed since the marriage was dissolved or annulled or;
-the existence of any pending proceedings between the parties for property adjustment orders under sections 23(a) or 24 of the M.C.A., or orders for financial relief under the C.A. or relating to the ownership of the dwelling home.

Where the applicant is a habitant or a cohabitant with no entitlement to occupy, additional circumstances to be taken into account are:
-the nature of parties to the relationship;
-the length of time during which they have lived together as husband and wife;
-whether there are or have been any children who are children of both parties or for whom they have or have had parental responsibilities.
The terms of the orders are the same as those available under section 33 of the FLA but the duration of the orders will differ. An order in respect of former spouses:
-may not be made after the death of either of the former spouses; and
-ceases to have effect on either of them;
-must be limited so as to have effect for a specified period not exceeding six months, but may be extended on one or more occasions for a further specified period not exceeding six months.

Applicant is a spouse, former spouse, a cohabitant or former cohabitant and neither applicant nor respondent has a right to occupy
Sections 37 and 38 of the F.L.A. deal with these situations, which are likely to be rare in practice. They deal with persons who occupy their home under contract with their employers or live in home owned by their parents, for example. Whatever their circumstances, the court is empowered to make orders in the same terms as under section 33 of the F.L.A.

Additional powers

Section 40(1)(a) of the Act provides that the court may, on making an order under ss 33, 35 or 36-or at any time thereafter-impose on either party obligations as to:

-the repair and maintenance of the dwelling house
-the discharge of rent
-the discharge of mortgage payments
-the discharge of other outgoings affecting the dwelling house.

It is anticipated that this power will be particularly useful when an occupation order continues for some time or while the outcome of the proceedings under the Matrimonial Causes Act 1973 is awaited.

The Law Commission also suggested that the court should have power to order an occupying party to make payments to the other for that occupation. Under the old law only the non-entitled spouse could be ordered to make such payments.

The Protection from Harassment Act 1997

This Act came into force on June 18th 1997. Although it is intended as a remedy against stalking, it is sufficiently wide to cover domestic situations as well. Section 1 provides that a person must not pursue a course of conduct that amounts to harassment of another and which he knows, or to know, amounts to harassment.

Section 2 creates a summary offence and section 4 an indictable offence where a person is put in fear of violence. The courts are empowered, in addition to other punishment, to issue restraining orders forbidding the offender from doing anything specified by the order for the purpose of protecting the victim. Further, section 3 creates a statutory tort of harassment and provides for the issue of injunctions, the breach of which entitles the plaintiff to apply for a warrant to arrest the defendant.

It is possible that this Act may be used to bypass non-molestation orders under the F.L.A. 1996 and injunctions under the inherent jurisdictions as well as being available to those who are not 'associated' with the defendant.

Enforcement

The matter of enforcement of these orders is always difficult. It is one thing to obtain an order and another to ensure that it is enforced.

In many cases, such orders are broken, and the topic of how to enforce obedience to such orders is very important indeed.

No court can directly force respondents to comply with such orders. Applicants must rely on the court's powers to punish respondents and hope that this, or the threat of it, will force compliance. Breach of an injunction granted either by the High Court or County Court is contempt and is punishable by either a fine or imprisonment.

To obtain the punishment of the respondent by either of these two methods, the applicant must take the responsibility for the institution and continuation of the process, a factor that can cause great stress and anxiety.

To avoid this, and the incurring of further costs by employing a solicitor, a power of arrest can be attached to injunctions and orders. The effect of this is that the police can arrest, without warrant, a person who has breached the order. The only initiative the applicant must take is to contact the police following the breach. The police must bring the person before the relevant court within 24 hours and the court can impose penalty.

As the arrest of an offender has dire consequences, the power of arrest attached to an order is usually hedged by limitations.

Domestic Violence, Crime and Victims Act 2004

Legislation has come into force as above, which has attempted to bridge the gap between the criminal and civil law relating to domestic violence. It inserts a new s 42A into the family Law Act 1996 and makes it a criminal offence to flout the civil orders relating to non-molestation, even where there is no power of arrest relating to the order. The Act makes common assault an arrestable offence, provides greater protection to victims during court hearings, improves sentencing of those convicted, establishes multi-agency reviews after familial killings, creates a register of offenders and aims to ensure that criminal and civil courts dealing with domestic violence liaise with each other.

New rules on coercive and controlling behaviour

In December 2014, it was announced that a new domestic abuse offence of coercive and controlling behaviour will come into force by late 2015. Coercive and controlling behaviour can include the abuser preventing their victims from having friendships or hobbies, refusing them access to money and determining tiny aspects of their everyday life, such as when they are allowed to sleep and go to the toilet etc.

Witness testimony could be supported at prosecution through documentary evidence, including threatening emails, text messages and bank statements that show the abuser has sought to control the victim financially.

Other steps

Steps which have been taken to try to ensure that domestic violence is dealt with more effectively include:

- The establishment of Specialist Domestic Violence Courts with specially trained magistrates and court officers
- Appointment of Independent Domestic Violence Advocates (IDVA's) who who work closely with victims to assess risk and discuss options
- Specially tailored programmes such as the Integrated Domestic Abuse programme (IDAP) developed by the National Offender Management Service (NOMS) as community order requirements for those convicted of domestic abuse offences
- Multi-agency Risk Assessment Conferences (MARAC's)

established in England and wales to coordinate responses of police, soical services, health, probation and education services to domestic abuse.

****

Ch. 8

Children and The Human Rights Act

The United Nations Convention on the rights of the child

The Convention transforms into legal obligations the affirmations on the Declaration of the Rights of the Child, which was adopted by the general assembly of the United Nations in 1959.

The Convention was ratified by the UK in 1991 but was taken into account when the Children Act 1989 was drafted. It is monitored by the Committee on the Rights of the Child, which makes suggestions and recommendation to governments and the general assembly on how the convention obligations can be met.

Definition of child

For the purposes of the UN Convention a child means, `every human being below the age of 18 years unless, under the law applicable to the child, majority is attained earlier'. The preamble to the Convention talks about the protection of the child before and after birth, but the UK Government entered a reservation limiting the application of the convention to children born alive. This means the Convention does not, in the UK, give the right to life for a foetus.

Fathers have no right to act as advocate for the foetus, because the foetus is regarded as not having individual rights

The main rights given by the Convention

- Article 2 - all the rights apply to all children, without discrimination on the basis of their race, colour, sex, language, religious, political or other opinion, national or social origin, property, disability, birth or other status.

- Article 3 - the best interest of the child shall be a primary consideration. The state is to provide adequate care when the family fails to do so.
- Article 6 - every child has an inherent right to life.
- Article 7 - every child has a right to a name from birth and to have a nationality
- Article 9 - a child has a right to live with his or her parents unless that is incompatible with his or her best interest, and the right to maintain contact with both parents if separated from them.
- Article 12 - the child has a right to express an opinion and have that opinion taken into account in accordance with his age and maturity.
- Article 13 - the child has a right to obtain and make known information and to express his or her views.
- Article 15 - children have a right to free association with others.
- Article 16 - they have a right to protection from interference with privacy, family, home and correspondence and from libel and slander.
- Article 18 - both parents have joint responsibility in bringing up their children and the state should support them in this task.
- Article 19 - the state has an obligation to protect children from all forms of maltreatment.
- Article 20 - the state has an obligation to provide special protection for children deprived of their family environment and to ensure an alternative family carer for them, taking into account their cultural background .Article 21 - adoption shall only be carried out in the best interest of the child,
- Article 22 - special protection is to be given to refugee children.

- Article 23 handicapped children are to receive special care, education and training to help them achieve the greatest possible self-reliance,
- Article 27 - children have a right to an adequate standard of living.
- Article 28-29 - they have a right to education and at least primary education should be free. Such education should be directed at developing the child's personality and talents, preparing the child for active life as an adult.
- Article 30 - children of minority communities and indigenous peoples have a right to enjoy their Own culture, religion and language.
- Article 31 - children have a right to leisure, play and participation in cultural activities.
- Article 32 - states must protect children from work which is a threat to their health, education or development.
- Article 33-36 - children have the right to be protected from drugs, sexual exploitation and abuse, trafficking and abduction and other forms of exploitation.
- Article 37 - no child shall be subjected to torture, cruel treatment, capital punishment, life imprisonment or unlawful deprivation of liberty
- Article 40 - child offenders have a right to due process of law.

The European Convention on Human Rights

The Human Rights Act 1998 incorporated, indirectly, the European Convention For the Protection of Fundamental Freedoms and Human Rights 1950 (ECHR) into UK law by requiring courts to interpret domestic law in a manner which is compatible with the convention. Accordingly, `human rights' issues may be raised by parties within all family proceedings. The domestic courts are not now bound by precedent created before the HRA 1998, but may reinterpret old law to ensure it is now compatible with the Convention. As an alternative, individuals who believe that their human rights have been breached by a public authority which has acted in a way incompatible with the Convention may sue under s7 and s8 of the HRA 1998.

Freestanding human rights applications in family cases

Freestanding applications against a public authority involve a more detailed investigation of the balancing exercise undertaken in the decision-making process than the alternative remedy of judicial review In HRA 1998 applications to the court must assess whether:

- an article of the Convention is engaged;
- it has been interfered with;
- the interference is in accordance with the law, and that law is reasonably foreseeable and accessible;
- the interference is in pursuit of a legitimate aim that interference is `necessary in a democratic society'. This means it must correspond to a `pressing social need' and is a `proportionate' response to the problem.
  The more serious the intervention the more compelling must be the justification

If there are existing care proceedings, human rights issues should be raised within those proceedings as all tiers of the family court system have jurisdiction under HRA 1998. After care orders are made, the parents and children continue to have a right to respect for their family life. Allegations of interference at this stage can be made as a freestanding civil application, or an application can be made under the CA 1989 and the human rights issues raised in those proceedings

A Local authority failure to protect children

A public authority has a positive duty to ensure that the rights of individuals are secured, as well as ensuring that its own acts were not incompatible with the convention. The European Court has held that the failure of a local authority to take into care four children who then suffered serious neglect and abuse amounted to inhuman and degrading treatment Similarly, leaving children in a home where a convicted abuser was known to reside and who subsequently abused the children was a breach of Article 3. The local authority should have investigated and taken steps to stop the abuse happening and to manage the case properly.

Procedural rights
The right to respect for family life means that parents must be involved in decision making to a degree which is sufficient to offer adequate procedural protection for their interests The right to a fair trial includes the ability to take issues relating to your civil rights to court, not merely being afforded a fair process when you get there.

Although there may be circumstances in which parents allege breaches of their rights after a care order is made but there is no relevant application available under the CA 1989, this does not make the CA 1989 incompatible with the Convention because the matter can be dealt with by way of freestanding application under s7 and s8 HRA 1998. A fair trial does not just comprise fairness at the judicial stage but fairness throughout the litigation process, and all documents and meetings must be open to all parties Individuals must be given the opportunity to contest the reliability; relevance or sufficiency of the information being compiled on them.

Procedural safeguards continue after the litigation is over. If there is to be a change in a care plan, parents must be told of the proposed changes and given the opportunity to make representations and to challenge the evidence on which the changes are based. The local authority is under a duty to make full and frank disclosure of all relevant information. Procedural flaws may not be sufficiently severe to affect the outcome of the case and justify a local authority's decision being set aside. Unless there are justifiable reasons to the contrary, a father without parental responsibility should be given leave to be joined in applications relating to his child to secure respect for his family life. Other applicants for leave to make applications under s8 CA

1989, such as grandparents, may also have Article 6 and 8 rights, and the minimum essential protection of these rights is that judges must be careful not to dismiss the applications without full inquiry

Proportionality of response
The actions of a local authority must be proportionate to the current risk of harm to the child concerned. Action must not be excessive or arbitrary. The lowest-level protective mechanisms must be used first. So removal of a child from a mother who was not currently mentally ill and who was in the controlled environment of a hospital was unjustified.

The local authority must look at the type of harm alleged and at the timescale within which it is thought likely that the risk will come to fruition when choosing protective measures If a supervision order would work because there was a level of parental cooperation and the risk of harm was at the low end of the spectrum, a care order which gave the local authority parental responsibility when they did not need it would be a disproportionate response. Balancing conflicting human rights, it may be necessary and proportionate to interfere with a parent's human rights to protect the human rights of a child, such as where granting a very late application by a father to be joined in proceedings would breach the child's right to a fair trial by causing undue delay.

In judicial decisions where the Article 8 rights of the parents and those of a child are at stake, the child's rights must be the paramount consideration. If any balancing of rights is necessary, those of the child must prevail.

****

Ch.9

Children And Adults

Parents Rights and obligations

Definition of a parent
The actual legal definition of a parent has been the subject of debate over the years. Whether the parent is a biological parent or psychological parent.

Biological parents
The law has traditionally approached the question of parentage by considering the biological link between adult and child as preferable. The law will rarely interfere with the authority of the biological parent, unless some other arrangement is preferable. In Re KD (a minor) (Ward: termination of access) 1988, Lord Templeman stated:

'The best person to bring up a child is the natural parent. It matters not whether the parent is wise or foolish, rich or poor, educated or illiterate, providing the child's moral and physical health is not endangered'.

There are two exceptions to this presumption: where the child is adopted (Adoption Act 1976 s39) and secondly where reproduction and childbirth follows on from sperm or egg donation (Human Fertilisation and Embryology Act 2008). Adoption will terminate the legal (parental) responsibility of natural parents towards the child and also extinguishes any rights a parent may have over a child. Where a person donates genetic material (eggs, sperm, embryos) he relinquishes any rights o biological parentage in relation to any child that may be born as a result.

Psychological parents

Good parenting depends very much on the ability to form an emotional/psychological bond with a child. A strong attachment between parent and child is considered to be an indicator of a stable and emotionally healthy relationship.

This bond is not exclusive to the biological parent but can form with a number of people, such as foster and adoptive parents. The courts have recognised the possibility of the independence of the biological and psychological relationship.

Parenting and the changing social context

During the last 50 years or so the family has undergone significant changes with respect to public perception and also the law. A number of aspects of the family need to be considered: socially acquired parentage, sexual orientation and parentage and multi-cultural family arrangements. With regard to socially acquired parentage, this refers to step-parents, a situation which will arise through either divorce or one-parent families resulting in remarriage. It can be said that the step parent will acquire the mantle of mother or father, with their role far more significant than the actual biological absent parent.

With regard to sexual orientation, whilst the heterosexual family remains the norm, homosexual men will father children and lesbian women will give birth to babies. They would also be considered parents. The assumption that homosexuals are not fit parents was challenged in Re W (Adoption: Homosexual Adopter) 1997, in which Singer J held that there was nothing in the Adoption Regulations to prevent a homosexual adopting a child and allowed a 49 year old lesbian woman in a settled relationship to adopt. The Adoption and Children Act 2002 (see adoption) has now authorised adoption by homosexual men and women.

With regards to multi-cultural family arrangements, patterns of immigration over the last 50 years have changed the family make up of the United Kingdom. In addition, the cultural make up of the country has changed and with it a need by the law to recognise and accept different cultural traditions.

The legal parent

A parent, in the eyes of the law is a person who has responsibility for a child. Parental responsibility means 'all the rights, duties, powers, responsibilities and authorities which by law a parent has in relation to the child and his property' (Children Act 1989 s3). Legal parenthood carries the right and responsibility to register a child's name within six months of its birth and apply for residence/contact orders, specific issue orders, change the child's name and to apply for a prohibited steps order to prevent the removal of the child from the country.

A parent is the natural mother or natural father of the child. However, not all fathers have parental responsibility for their child and other parties may also have parental responsibility for the child. In addition, the local authority may have parental responsibility for the child where the child is in care, and foster parents may have responsibility. More than one person can have parental responsibility for a child (CA 1989 s 2(5)). Where other parties have parental responsibility for the child, this will only last for the duration of the order made in their favour.

Parental responsibility

Any person who is a legal parent has parental responsibility. In accordance with the Children Act 1989, s2, more than one person may have responsibility for the child at any one time. Thus, parental responsibility is shared in the case of a married couple and is shared where parents are separated. In cases where children are taken into care, the natural parents will still have parental responsibility: the responsibility will simply be shared with foster parents.

The following outlines who has parental responsibility:

- The mother has automatic parental responsibility (whether a child is born within or out of marriage s 33 Human Fertilisation and Embryology Act 2008);
- The married father;
- The unmarried father has automatic responsibility if the Adoption and Children Act 2002 s111(2)(a)(c) applies;
- The unmarried father if he is granted a court order under the Children Act 1989, s4;
- The adoptive parents of an adoptive child;
- If a child is a ward of court the court stands in the position of parents and a court in wardship has parented responsibility;
- A guardian appointed by a parent by deed or will has parental responsibility after the parents death;
- The Children's Act 1989 created the institution of custodianship, under which many parental rights are given to the foster parent but some rights remain with the natural parent.

Proving parentage

In cases where the identity of the biological father is unknown and the mother wishes to establish parentage, or the child or father wishes to dispute parentage, an order for a declaration of paternity (under the Family Law Act) 1986, s55A, as amended by the Child Support, Pensions and Social Security Act 2000, s83(2) may be made. However, blood testing will only be ordered if it is considered to be in the child's best interests. In re O; Re J (children) (Blood Tests: Constraint) (2000) in two separate cases, a male applicant had obtained an order under s 20 (1) of the Family Law Reform Act 1969 for the use of blood tests designed to determine the paternity of a child who was the subject of the proceedings. In each case, the mother, whose consent was required under s 21(3) of the 1969 Act, refused to consent to the child's blood being tested. The court held that it was a matter for the mother to grant or withhold consent.

The courts, however, can order a blood test to be taken if it considers this to be in the best interests of child.

Step-parents

Where a parent remarries, the new spouse becomes the step-parent of any children of the previously married partner. Under the Adoption and Children's Act 2002, amending the Children's Act 1989 s 4(A)1:

Where a child's parent (A) who has parental responsibility for the child is married to a person who is not the child's parent (step parent) (a) parent A or, if the other parent of the child also has parental responsibility for the child, both parents may, by agreement with the step-parent provide for the step-parent to have parental responsibility for the child or (b) the court may, on application of the step-parent, order that the step-parent shall have parental responsibility for the child.

The Civil Partnership Act 2004 provides that civil partners will be eligible to apply for parental responsibility on the same basis as step parents.

Adoptive parents

An order of the court placing a child for adoption establishes the adoptive parent as the legal parent. The ACA 2002, s 46(1) states:

1) an adoption order is an order made by the court on an application under s 50 or 51 giving parental responsibility for a child to the adopters or adopter.
2) The making of an adoption order operates to extinguish the parental responsibility which any person other than the adopters or adopter has for the adopted child immediately before the making of the order.

Foster parents

When a child is in care of the local authority, he or she will be placed with foster carers. This can be a single adult or an adult couple in a family arrangement.

Parents and reproductive technology

The Human Fertilisation and Embryology Act 2008 came into effect on 13th November 2008 and amends the HFEA 1990. The key provisions of the 2008 Act are to:

- Ensure that all human embryos outside the body-whatever the process used in their creation-are subject to regulation.
- Ensure regulation of "human-admixed" embryos created from a combination of human and animal genetic material for research.
- Ban sex-selection of offspring for non-medical reasons. Sex selection is allowed for medical reasons.
- Recognise same sex couples as legal parents of children conceived through the use of donated sperm, eggs or embryos.
- Retain a duty to take account of the welfare of the child in providing fertility treatment, but replace the reference to "the need for a father" with the "need for supportive parenting"-hence valuing the role of all parents.
- Alter the restrictions on the use of HFEA-collected data to help enable follow up research of infertility treatment.

Under the Human Fertilisation and Embryology Act (HFEA) 2008, where a person has donated sperm or eggs then he or she relinquishes any rights over the genetic material. The HFEA determines the legal parent as a result of a child born from IVF treatment. The HFEA 2008, defines a 'mother' as 'the woman who is carrying or who has carried a child as a result of the placing in her of an embryo, or of sperm or eggs'.

Section 28 defines a father as being married to the woman 'at the time of placing in her of an embryo or the sperm or the eggs or of her insemination' unless it is shown that he did not consent to the placing in her of the embryo, sperm or eggs or to her insemination.

The Human Fertilisation and Embryology Authority (Disclosure of Donor) Regulations 2004

These regulations were passed to acknowledge a child's rights to know their genetic parentage. This is an important part of a child's identity. However, correspondingly, there is no obligation on the parents to tell the child that they were conceived using donated sperm.

Parties separating

When parties who consented to the placement of genetic material in the woman separate, a specific legal position arises. In the case of Re R (a child) (IVF Paternity of Child) 2005, the mother, A, and her partner B, were unmarried and sought IVF treatment which involved the fertilisation of A's eggs with sperm from a donor. In accordance with IVF procedure, B signed a form acknowledging that he would be the father of any child born in consequence. However, A nd B had already separated when implementation in A had taken place, about which B had no knowledge. On an application by B, the judge declared under HFEA 1990, s28(3) that B was the legal father of the resulting child.

The court of appeal allowed A's appeal. B appealed and the House of Lords dismissed the ruling of the court of appeal holding:

'that section 28(3) of the HFEA should only apply to cases falling clearly within it and the legal relationship of a parent should not be based on a fiction, especially where deception was involved: that the embryo had to have been placed in the woman when treatment services were provided for her and the man together; and that, although they had originally been so provided for A and B, they had not been when implementation took place'.

Parental responsibility and childrens rights generally
Rights of Children in Domestic and International Law

The dominant statute governing the position of children in the UK is the Children Act 1989. This act sets out the fundamental premise of decisions taken in relation to children, which is the welfare principle. This provides that where decisions involving children are to be taken, the best interests of the children are the paramount consideration. The welfare principle has historically guided the development of children's law in the UK, and is the most significant restriction on children's autonomy and ability to exercise their rights independently. It is addressed in more detail below.

Further to the government's 'Every Child Matters' agenda, The Children's Act (CA) 2004 received royal assent in November 2004. The 2004 act codified 'five outcomes' for children, being their rights to:

- Be healthy

- Stay safe

- Enjoy and achieve

- Make a positive contribution

- Achieve economic well-being

The CA 2004 created a Children's Commissioner, and imposed enforceable duties on local authorities and other relevant bodies such as the police, NHS health services etc to work together in the provision of children's services.

Every Children's Services Authority (local authority) is required to publish a Children and Young People's Plan. This plan should show how the authority intends to enable children in their area to meet the five outcomes, and must be regularly reviewed. The European Convention on Human Rights (ECHR) has been incorporated into UK law, and is relevant to the rights of children and young people in much the same way as it is to those of adults. In addition, where the ECHR rights of a competent child are infringed simply by reason of their being a child, the anti-discrimination provisions in Article 14 may be applicable.

Office of the Children's Commissioner

The general function of the Office of the Children's Commissioner (OCC) is to promote the awareness of the views and the interests of children. The OCC is the only statutory body with a stated duty to have regard to the provisions of the UNCRC.

The OCC cannot undertake casework on behalf of children or investigate individual cases. However, it can act as a referral body for cases which fall within the remit of the newly created Commission for Equality and Human Rights.

The OCC is in the process of establishing a scheme to conduct 'child impact assessments' on proposed UK legislation. The aim of these assessments will be to provide an analysis of likely effect of the legislation on the rights and interests of children and young people. The weight that Parliament will give such assessments remains to be seen.

Key Areas of Parental Responsibility

Consultation with Children

Parents (and others exercising parental responsibility) are not legally obliged to consult their children as to their wishes or to involve them in decision making processes.

However, the exercise of parental responsibility is limited when children have sufficient understanding and capacity to make decisions about their own future. This was confirmed in the 1985 decision in *Gillick v Wisbeach Health Authority*, in which the House of Lords decided that a child under 16 could consent to medical treatment if he or she could understand what was involved in such treatment and was capable of expressing his or her views and wishes. This has come to be known as 'Gillick competence' and while the House of Lords did not identify a specific age at which children were to be deemed to be sufficiently mature to have their views considered, it follows from Gillick that the older the child, the greater the weight that will be attached to their views. This approach is consistent with certain provisions of the UNCRC – Article 5 which requires that children's rights be exercised in accordance with their evolving capacities and Article 12 which requires that in all decisions effecting children due weight should be attached to their views.

In 2006 the High Court applying Gillick, confirmed that young people were entitled to confidential advice or treatment on sexual matters, which includes abortion, without the knowledge or consent of their parents. This position does not breach the child's parent's rights to private and family life under Article 8 ECHR.

Names

A child's parents have an unfettered right to name their child and are required by law to register the child's name within 42 days of the child's birth. Where only one person has parental responsibility that person can change the child's name (e.g by deed poll) without requiring the consent or permission of anyone else. Where there is more than one person with parental responsibility and dispute as to change of name then it will be necessary to seek the court's permission. The court will consider a range of factors but the paramount consideration will be the welfare of the child. The opinions of a older child are likely to be highly relevant. A change of name is considered to be serious step, relating as it does to a child's identity.

Where a child becomes the subject of an adoption order, the adoptive parents acquire parental responsibility and have an absolute right to change a child's name.

With parental consent a child may use a different name from that on their birth certificate. A child of sixteen may change their name without their parent's consent. (A parent may apply to court in an attempt to prevent this but is unlikely to be successful). Equally, a child with sufficient maturity and understanding who is under the age of sixteen may apply to the court for permission.

Religion

A child who is sufficiently mature in accordance with the Gillick principles is entitled to choose his or her own religion. Where a dispute arises either between parents or between parents and the child over the choice of religious upbringing, the paramountcy of the child's welfare will prevail in resolving the conflict. If a parent seeks to impose a particular religion on a child it will not be tolerated if it causes harm to the child. Article 9 of the ECHR protects the right to freedom of thought, conscience and religion. (See also education, below).

Medical Treatment

In most cases it will be the parents who consent to medical treatment on behalf of their child. A child/young person can give valid consent provided the person providing treatment is of the view that he or she understands the nature and consequences of the treatment (ie that they are Gillick competent). At the time of writing the General Medical Council were seeking the views of children and young people in order to draft guidance to doctors as to the treatment of children.

Children under 18 may also refuse medical treatment but under the wardship jurisdiction a court can order medical treatment, including termination of a pregnancy or sterilisation, if it is deemed necessary in the child's best interests. This power is most commonly used in cases where a young person refuses life saving medical treatment due as a consequence of an eating disorder or mental illness.

The ECHR has decided that compulsory medical treatment for the purposes of preventing death or serious injury does not amount to inhuman or degrading treatment contrary to Article 3 ECHR where a patient is not capable of giving consent.

Consent to Marriage

There is no specific criminal offence of forced marriage, although the Foreign and Commonwealth Office deal with cases of UK children as young as 13 being forced into marriage.

A marriage where one party is under 16 is void. Young people between 16 and 18 may marry with parental consent. If the parents are separated or divorced the consent of both parents is necessary and if the child is in the care of the local authority it is necessary to obtain the consent of all persons having parental responsibility for the child.

Article 12 of the Convention protects the right of men and women of 'marriageable age' to marry. The prohibition on the marriage of children under 16 years does not infringe the right to marry because Article 12 clearly permits states to regulate the age at which a person is able to marry. Similarly, it is not possible to enter into a civil partnership if under the age of 16. A young person of 16 or 17 may only register a civil partnership with the consent of their parents.

Corporal Punishment

In international law physical punishment of children is totally prohibited. However, in the UK parents still have the right to administer reasonable physical chastisement to a child. It is possible to defend a charge of common assault against a child on the basis that the force used was no more than reasonable punishment. This position has been strongly criticised by the UN Committee, and by the Children's Commissioners for England, Wales, Scotland and Northern Ireland, who in 2006 issued a joint statement condemning the UK's position and calling for an outright ban on the physical punishment of children.

Corporal punishment is prohibited as a form of punishment in all other circumstances including as a punishment following conviction for an offence, in education and in care or foster homes.

In 2005 the UK House of Lords held that the ban on corporal punishment in independent schools did not amount to a breach of the parents' rights under Articles 8 and 9 ECHR. Parliament was bound to respect a religious belief in corporal punishment in school, but entitled to legislate in children's best interests against the manifestation of that belief.

Leaving Home

Generally, young people under 16 cannot leave home unless their parents agree.. The law relating to 16 to 17 year olds is not clear but it

96

appears that they probably can leave home without parental consent. In theory, parents can apply to court for the return home of a child under 18 by seeking an injunction in wardship proceedings or a residence order. However, a court is extremely unlikely to order a child of 16 to 17 to return home against his or her wishes.

A court may make a residence order in favour of another adult if this is deemed to be in the child's best interests. This can be done on the adult's application or by the child if he or she is deemed to have sufficient understanding. The leave of the court is required,

Police will return a runaway child under 16 to his or her parents or to the local authority if he or she is in care unless they have reasonable cause to believe the child is in danger or at risk. In such circumstances the police may hold the child in police protection. The police then liaise with social services as to whether further action should be taken to protect the child. The police are unlikely to return a child over the age of 16 to his or her parents.

Ages of Consent

The legal definition of childhood remains quite fluid, and while children do not acquire full independence until they reach the age of 18 they can legally engage in certain adult activities before that age.

At 16 a young person can consent to sex, join the armed services (although they will not generally be deployed on active service until they are 18) and get married with their parent's consent. Whereas 16 year olds have traditionally been able to buy cigarettes, in October 2007 the minimum age rose to 18.

The Children Act 1989 aims to encourage parents to agree about the child's welfare in the event of separation or divorce by providing for the continuation of parental responsibility for divorced parents and by requiring the courts to refrain from making orders unless they are desirable in the child's best interests (the 'no order' principle). This approach is reinforced by the development of conciliation and mediation processes to assist parents to reach agreement.

Where there is agreement between parents they are not required to attend court in divorce proceedings in relation to the children. The court must simply be satisfied that appropriate arrangements have been made for children having received a written declaration to that effect and the divorce is granted. In cases where the court is concerned about the plans for the children it can order a welfare report but this power is very rarely used. However it is concerning that in an uncontested case there is no formal way in which children can express their views if they wish to do so.

In 2001 the Children and Family Court Advisory and Support Service (CAFCASS) was established. CAFCASS has a number of functions. In this context the most important is the provision of Child and Family Reporter to carry out conciliation and reporting functions in disputes between parents over residence and contact.

Parents making applications for residence or contact with a child may be required to attend a conciliation appointment with a mediator or child and family reporter. The purpose of the conciliation stage is to assist the parties to resolve their disputes. If this is not possible then the Court may order a report to be prepared on the matter of residence or contact. A child and family reporter involved at the conciliation plays no further part in the process and does not participate in the preparation of any reports for the court.

In addition to applications for residence and contact, which are made under section 8 of the Children Act 1989, parents can also apply for a specific issue order requiring a particular action by another parent or for a prohibited steps order to prevent a parent from taking certain steps, for example removing a child from the other parents care and control. Section 8 applications often involve the use of child and family reporters to provide the court with an objective assessment of what is in the child's best interests. Children and young people may apply to court for section 8 orders provided they can demonstrate sufficient maturity and understanding. However, the court does not have to grant a child leave, and retains a discretion to refuse an application of a competent child. (see chapter 11 for more on different order).

Welfare Principle

The concept of welfare is not defined in the Children Act 1989 but the following factors which constitute the 'welfare checklist' are used to assist the Court in its determination:

- The ascertainable wishes and feelings of the child – in light of his or her age and understanding;

- The physical, emotional and educational needs of the child;

- The likely effect of any change on the child's circumstances;

- The age, sex, background and any other characteristics which the court considers to be relevant;

- Any harm which the child has suffered or is at risk of suffering;

- How capable the child's parents (and/or any other relevant person) are of meeting the child's needs; and

- The range of powers available to the court.

The child and family reporter is also required to take the welfare checklist into account in the preparation of his or her report.

Article 8 of the ECHR – the right to respect for family life – impacts on this decision making process in that a court must be aware of the parents' right to respect for their family life. The courts have taken the view that while a balance must be struck between the competing interests of parents and children, the welfare principle continues to predominate under the Children Act 1989.

In most cases such children will not participate directly but will be represented by a children's guardian appointed by CAFCASS. Most children's guardians have worked as social workers but they are appointed to act independently and to represent the child's interests.

Contact Disputes

The question of how much contact a child should have with a non-residential parent is a difficult matter for the court to resolve to the satisfaction of the parents and the child. Under the Children Act 1989 contact is expressed as a right of the child although the ECHR has recognised it as an element of a parent's family life. In striking a balance between the competing interests the courts are guided by considerations of the child's welfare as the paramount consideration but the view in the vast majority of cases is that maintaining a relationship with both parents is in the child's best interests. Terminating direct contact between a child and a non residential parent is a rare occurrence and usually only happens where there has been violence or abuse of an extreme nature or where for other reasons the child does not wish to continue to have a relationship with his or her parents.

Children and the Criminal Justice system

More recently, the Children and Adoption Act 2006 has given the courts greater powers to enforce orders for contact (although at the time of writing these have not yet come into force).

Under section 37 of the Crime and Disorder Act 1998 (CDA) the principal aim of the youth justice system is to prevent offending by children and young persons. The CDA seeks to achieve this aim by promoting a range of diversionary tactics which remove children from the criminal justice system and introducing a range of alternative sentences if children are thought to be acting in an anti social manner. The use of such measures however is controversial because they effectively create status offences where behaviour which would not attract criminal sentences if it were committed by adults is criminalised in respect of children.

Criminal Responsibility

Children below the age of ten cannot be charged with criminal offences as they are considered incapable of committing criminal offences. This is considerably lower than the age in most other countries and in both 1995 and 2002 the UN Committee recommended that the age of criminal responsibility be raised. Under the CDA, children under the age of ten can be the subject of a Child Safety Order. The order has the effect of placing the child under the supervision of a social worker or the youth offending team and it may require a child to comply with certain conditions such as curfews.

Another new measure introduced by the CDA is the introduction of Local Curfew Schemes which allow the Local Authority in consultation with the Home Office to introduce a scheme whereby children are banned from being in a public place during certain hours unless they are accompanied by an adult. Police can take a child home and inform the local authority if they are of the view that the child breached the order. The local authority has an obligation to follow up on any breach by making its own enquiries. This scheme was originally intended to apply to children under ten but can now be used for older children as well.

A further initiative of the CDA is the Anti Social Behaviour Order (ASBO) which can be used on any person over the age of ten years. The local authority or the police can make an application to a Magistrates' Court for an ASBO where it appears that a person or family is behaving in a manner which has caused or is likely to cause harassment, alarm or distress to a person or people not of the same household. This is a civil application and the onus is on the defendant to disprove the allegations. ASBOs can last up to two years and a breach of an ASBO is a criminal offence.

In 2005 the CDA was amended to allow Parental Compensation Orders to be granted in relation to the behaviour of children under the age of 10 (there is no minimum age). Under these measures a parent can be fined up to £5,000 for the behaviour of their children.

The CDA also removed the concept of 'doli incapax' under which children between the ages of ten to 13 were deemed incapable of knowing the difference between right and wrong. These children are now treated the same as other young people aged 14 to 17 years.

The rules for police questioning, search and detention of young people are the same as for adults but young people have additional rights. Parents must be informed of the arrest and detention and interviews should only take place in the presence of an appropriate adult. The appropriate adult can be a parent, guardian, social worker or other responsible adult aged at least 18. The role of the appropriate adult is unclear but they should be able to advise and assist the juvenile and to ensure the interview is conducted fairly.

When it is a first offence the police have the discretion to issue a reprimand instead of proceeding with prosecution. For a second offence a warning may be used. A second warning may only be issued if the latest offence is not serious and more than two years have elapsed since the making of the first warning. Reprimands and warnings can only be given if the young person admits the offence, has no previous convictions and it is considered contrary to the public interest for the offender to be prosecuted. Reprimands and warnings are made at the police station in the presence of the appropriate adult. Following a warning the young person is referred to the Youth Offending Team for an assessment to decide whether a rehabilitation programme is appropriate. Reprimands and warnings do not form part of a person's criminal record although they may be brought if there are court proceedings in the future.

Criminal trials

The majority of young people are tried in Youth Court. This is a specialist branch of the Magistrate's Court. Certain serious offences such as murder, manslaughter, rape, arson, aggravated burglary and robbery are heard in the Crown Court. In both courts there is a requirement that the welfare of the child is considered when sentencing but this is a weaker requirement than in the family courts. Following a decision of the ECHR guidance was issued to remind judges of the importance of guaranteeing the fair trial rights of young people in accordance with Article 6. In particular they are required to ensure that children sit with their lawyers and understand the nature of the proceedings and the evidence which is being given against them. In addition judges are required to provide regular breaks and to restrict reporting in the media where appropriate.

Sentencing
Community sentences
In common with adults, young people may be subject to a range of sentences including a fine, attendance order or supervision order. Supervision orders may include a range of conditions such as participation in particular activities, night restrictions or a requirement that the child lives in social services accommodation for up to 6 months. New sentences under the CDA include reparation orders and action plan orders. These are intended to provide young people with the opportunity to avoid custodial sentences and to make amends to victims or to the community.

Referral orders are similar and were introduced by the Criminal Justice and Youth Evidence Act 1999. It is aimed at the first time offender who admits the offence and where the offence would only normally attract a fine. It allows the juvenile to be referred to the Youth Offending team and work is carried out to challenge their behaviour.

Children in Detention
Custodial Sentence
The CDA introduced the detention and training order for young people between the ages of 12 and 17 years. The sentence is intended to be divided between a custodial stage and a training stage. It is available for 15 to 17 year olds if they are convicted of an offence which is so serious that only custody is appropriate and they are persistent offenders, or for 12 to 14 year olds who are convicted of a serious offence and the court is of the view that custody is appropriate and again they are persistent offenders. It can also be available for 11 to 12 year olds if made available by the Home Secretary where the child is found to be a persistent offender and custody is deemed necessary to

protect the public. The training half of the sentence is supervised and it is intended to provide skills aimed at rehabilitation. This sentence can be made for 24 months provided that it does not exceed the adult sentence available for the offence.

Detention at Her Majesty's Pleasure

Young offenders convicted under the age of 18 of murder may be detained at Her Majesty's pleasure which is indefinite detention firstly in social services secure accommodation transferring at 18 to a young offender institution and at 21 to prison. The length of detention is however set by the Lord Chief Justice and it is for the Parole Board to determine whether the young person should be released.

Detention under section 53 of the Children and Young Person Act 1933

Young offenders under the age of 18 convicted of grave crimes which would attract a period of imprisonment of 14 years or more if committed by an adult may be convicted to a period of detention for periods in excess of 24 months provided that the sentence does not exceed the maximum term which would be imposed if an adult committed the offence. The court should determine the appropriate sentence for rehabilitation and deterrence and for young people this is normally one half of the sentence before referral is made to the parole board. Young people are referred to the Parole Board for a determination as to whether it is safe to release the young person on licence once the tariff period has expired.

Conditions of Detention

The UK government ratified the UNCRC with a reservation in relation to Article 37 (that wherever it is necessary for children to be detained, they should be held separately from adults). While progress in this area has been made, the UK retains this reservation and increasing prison numbers may mean that children are again detained in adult facilities.

In 2006 the Carlile Inquiry reported on the routine use of strip-searching, restraint and segregation against children in custody. The report called for greater safeguards for children in custody and stated that may of the practices would be regarded as child abuse in any other setting. In particular, the use of painful 'distraction' techniques may raise issues under Articles 3 and 8 of the ECHR.

In a recent decision (2007) the High Court has confirmed the existence of a duty on Social Services departments to assess the needs of detained children where there is a real prospect of their release from detention.

Education

While education is recognised as a right of the child, international and domestic human rights law have tended to focus disproportionately on the rights of parents to control the content of their children's education. For example, Article 2, Protocol 1 of the Convention states that everyone has a right to education and then goes on to say that the State has an obligation to respect the rights of parents to ensure that education and teaching of their children is in conformity with the parents' religious and philosophical convictions. The emphasis on the rights of parents as consumers in education law and policy is problematic because it dilutes the child's right to an education and it discourages acceptance of children's right to participate. The Joint Committee on Human Rights has expressed concerns about the inadequacy of recent education legislation, in light of Article 12 UNCRC.

The law governing education in England and Wales is complex not least because there is a range of different types of state maintained schools, independent (albeit state funded) schools such as Academies and City Technology Colleges, and fully independent schools . Further, the Education and Inspections Act 2006 allowed schools to become Trust (foundation) schools.

Compulsory education

Children over the age of five and under the age of 16 are of compulsory education age and they must receive full time education. Parents are required to ensure that a child receives efficient full-time education suitable to his or her age, ability and aptitude and to ensure that any special educational needs are met by attendance at school or otherwise. Parents may educate children at home or engage a private tutor, but the Local Education Authority (LEA) must be satisfied that the education is of a sufficiently high standard. If the LEA are concerned that a child is not receiving a suitable education other than at school they may serve formal notice on the parents requiring them to satisfy the LEA otherwise. Where the parents fail to do so, the LEA can serve a School Attendance Order (SAO) requiring the parents to register the child at a named school. Parents must be given notice of the LEA's intention to serve this order and the named school must not be one from which the child has been excluded.

The SAO lasts while the child is of compulsory school age unless it is repealed by a court order. Where a parent fails to comply with the SAO s/he can be prosecuted before a Magistrates' Court and can be fined up to £1000. Where a parent knows that a child is not attending school and fails to take steps to make the child attend, the parent can be fined up to £2500 or imprisoned for not more than three months. A court which has convicted a parent for a failure to comply with a SAO can direct the LEA to apply for an Education Supervision Order. The LEA does not have to do this but it must tell the court why it has chosen not to make an application.

The purpose of an Education Supervision Order is to guide parents and children to ensure that the children receive a satisfactory education. The Department of Health has issued guidance on the use of Education Supervision Orders which last for up to one year initially, but may be extended for up to three years at a time. They cannot last beyond the point at which the child is no longer of compulsory school age.

Special Educational Needs

LEA's must make special provision for children who have learning disabilities to ensure that they are provided with education which meets their needs. The general preference is that children with special educational needs (SEN) remain in mainstream schools.

Schools have an obligation to ensure that a child's special educational needs are identified and known to those involved in teaching the child. This process is done by way of assessment and a child who has SEN is 'statemented' – a statement of the child's needs and measures which are to be taken to deal with those needs is provided. If parents are not satisfied with the eventual provisions or the nominated school, they may appeal to a Special Educational Needs Tribunal provided that they require the assessment of the child themselves. The question of whether a child requires assessment and statementing can often be contentious in that parents may wish to have a child statemented but can encounter considerable difficulties in convincing a school to undertake this process.

Where the school refuses to statement a child the parents can appeal to the SEN tribunal. Each school is required to have a Special Education Needs Co-ordinator (SENCO) who is responsible for overseeing the provision of SEN for a child within the school.

Parenting Contracts and Orders

An LEA or school governing body can apply to the magistrates' court for a parenting order covering the parents of a child who has been excluded from school. The relevant exclusion must have been either permanent or for two fixed periods within twelve months. A parenting order requires the parent to exercise control over the child, and to attend counselling or a guidance programme. Parents who fail to keep to the terms of a parenting order are guilty of a criminal offence, and could be fined.

Parenting contracts are a new provision allowing for formal agreements between parents and the school or LEA, which codify the intended action in relation to a specific child's attendance and behaviour.

Employment

No one under 16 can legally be employed in work other than light work, or undertake any work which is likely to be harmful to their safety, health, development, or that will affect their attendance at school or participation in work experience. Children under the age of 14 can only be employed in specific areas.

Specific rules in any given area will be governed by local authority by-laws. Employers who want to employ children or young people under school leaving age are required to get a permit from their local authority. The permit must be signed by both the employer and one of the child's parents. There are strict rules as to how many hours a young person under 16 can legally work. A person of compulsory school age must not work more than two hours on a school day, or more than twelve hours in any week when s/he is attending school.

Under 16 year olds are not entitled to the National Minimum Wage, nor to paid holiday, and young people over 16 but under 22 receive a lower Minimum Wage. The UN Committee have expressed concern that this discriminates against the most A child born in the UK before 1 January 1983 is automatically a British citizen irrespective of the nationality of his or her parents. Children born in the UK after that date are entitled to British Citizenship only if one parent is a British Citizen or is settled in the UK at the time of their birth. In July 2006 the law was amended to allow unmarried to transmit their nationality to their children in the same way as married fathers.

Citizenship

A child who is not a British Citizen but is adopted by British Citizens becomes entitled to citizenship from the time of the adoption order.

The OCC has raised concerns that children who are British citizens are effectively being expelled from the UK in circumstances in which the parent with care is a third country national without leave to remain. vulnerable workers.

Travelling and Leaving the Country

Since October 1998 all children who were not on a valid 10-year passport need to have a passport of their own to travel abroad. A parent or other person with a residence order may take a child out of the country for a period of four weeks without the permission of non-residential parents or other holders of parental responsibility. This is to allow parents to take their children for holidays without requiring permission of the other parent. However where a parent is concerned about the frequency of such trips or has fears that a parent may abduct a child he or she can apply to the court to impose restrictions on removal or require that a passport be surrendered.

Removal of a child from the jurisdiction on a more permanent basis is more complicated. Again the paramountcy of the child's welfare will prevail in considering whether such a move should be permitted. A court will also consider the impact of the removal on the child's relationship with his or her other parent and any siblings or extended family members who are to remain in the UK.

Where a child is removed from the jurisdiction without agreement it is possible to use the Hague Conventions on Child Abduction (the Hague Conventions), which provide a procedure for the summary return of abducted children. The aim is that the law of the country of habitual residence of the child should be enforced unless specific and somewhat restrictive grounds can be satisfied that the courts in the country of habitual residence should sort out any difficulties that need resolution. While courts must take into account the wishes and feelings of the child, children do not have a right to invoke the Hague Conventions in their own right.

Access to Justice and Redress

A *Gillick* competent child (see chapter on Rights of adolescents) is entitled to instruct a solicitor in their own right. Where public funding (legal aid) is available a child will be entitled to make an application for such funding in the same way as an adult. Where the child is under 16

109

the Legal Services Commission will normally expect an application on behalf of a child to be made by an adult acting on the child's behalf. If there are no suitable adults an application can be made by the child in person.

A child will be the appropriate applicant for legal aid where the legal problem relates to them and/or they have standing to bring an action. In certain areas, where an appeal right vests in a child's parent (such a school admission appeals: see above) the Legal Services Commission will not view a child as an appropriate applicant for funding, notwithstanding that their rights are affected.

An action under the Human Rights Act 1998 can only be brought by a victim or would-be victim of the alleged violation. Where a child is the victim of an alleged HRA breach, a parent will not have standing to bring the action and a child should not be refused funding on the basis that an adult could fund/bring the action in their place.

On a child's application for public funding it is their own means that will be taken into account. All applications, be subject to a consideration as to whether there are alternative sources of funding available; this could include consideration of a child's parent's financial circumstances, and a judgement may be made that it would be reasonable for a parent/guardian to seek advice and/or bring any action in their own name, rather than through the child.

The Civil Procedure Rules require a child to conduct proceedings through a litigation friend. However a child can apply to the court for an order that they be allowed to conduct proceedings without a litigation friend (CPR part 21).

****

Ch.10

Adoption

The Adoption and Children Act 2002 (ACA 2002)

The central objective of adoption is now aimed at providing a stable and permanent future in a family for children who are being cared for by the local authority. The ACA 2002 (amended by the Children and Adoption Act 2006-see below) and also amended by the Children and Families Act 2014, introduced some significant improvements to existing adoption law. The main aim is to ensure that the welfare of the child is paramount (ACA 2002 s 1(2). Courts must apply this test when considering an adoption order. Also, the courts can dispense with the consent of existing parents if the welfare of the child requires it.

The 2002 ACA also recognises the geopolitics of family life-that for many children maintaining contact with birth parents is of the utmost importance. With this in mind, ACA s1 (4) (f) requires courts to consider:

'the relationship the child has with relatives, and with any other person in relation to whom the court or agency considers the relationship to be relevant, including:

(i)   the likelihood of any such relationship continuing and the value to the child of its doing so;

(ii)   the ability and willingness of any of the child's relatives, or of any such person to provide the child with a secure environment in which the child can develop, and otherwise to meet the child's needs;

(iii)   the wishes and feelings of any of the child's relatives, or of any such person, regarding the child.

This represents a significant departure from previous adoption law which was to sever all ties with the birth family. The ACA 2002 s 1(5) required that in placing the child for adoption, the agency must give due consideration to the child's religious persuasion, racial origin and cultural and linguistic background. However, the Children and Families Act 2014 s 3 repeals this requirement (in England but not in Wales).

Whilst working towards acquiring the consent of the natural parents to adoption remains a priority (ACA 2002 s19(1) dispensing with consent has now been simplified and is permitted if the welfare of the child requires it, or the natural parents cannot be found or are incapable of giving consent.

The ACA 2002 abolished the freeing order and introduced a placement order which can only be made if the parents have consented or if their consent may be dispensed with.

The ACA 2002 recognises that contemporary families may not be monogamous or heterosexual. However, stability and permanence in a relationship is recognised as of paramount importance. Unmarried couples can now adopt. This also includes homosexual couples following the passing of the Civil Partnerships Act 2004. Single persons can also adopt. However, a single homosexual man may not be seen as suitable as a single heterosexual.

In Frette v France 2003, a single homosexual man applied for prior authorization to adopt. His sexual orientation was a decisive factor in the courts refusal. The court took the view that the applicants lifestyle did not appear to be such as to provide sufficient guarantees that he would be able to provide a suitable home for the child.

Step-parents can now acquire parental responsibility through a 'parental order' rather than adoption.

The ACA 2002 also introduces a new status of ' special guardianship' where total severance from the birth family is not appropriate and the possibility of contact with birth parents pertains.

Once an adoption order is made, adoption is final. Adoption terminates, once and for all, the parental responsibility of the natural parent.

Adoption services

Under the ACA 2002, only a local authority or a registered adoption society can provide adoption services. The latter must be registered under the National Care Standards Commission. Under s4 (1) of the act 'adoption agencies' have responsibility for selecting and assessing adopters and placing children for adoption. This includes the provision of support services, discussed below. S5 states that local authorities must prepare a clear adoption plan for the provision of services with regard to the adoption of the child. Section 109 requires the court to draw up a plan with a view to determining applications.

The Adopted Children Register And The Adoption Contact Register

The Adopted Children Register is a register of adoptions taking place in England & Wales and is kept in the General Register Office, but the Register itself is not open to public inspection or search. However, the index of the Register is available for inspection and anyone can apply on payment of a fee for a certified copy of an entry in the register relating to a child who has reached 18.

An adopted person can apply to obtain a copy of their birth certificate but the Local Authority must make the application.

The Adopted Contact Register is also a register kept at the General register office and again the register itself is not available for public inspection and search but it is possible to apply for certified copies of entries in the register. The register contains information about adopted persons who have given notice expressing a wish to make contact with their relatives and who have reached 18.

Opening up of adoption information

From December 2013, families have a greater say in selecting which child to adopt under radical new measures. Couples are able to check online which councils can best help them find a child, instead of being limited to their local authority. From 2014, families approved for adoption are also be able to browse profiles of thousands of children waiting for a new home. Access to the adoption register has previously been the preserve of social workers who decide on parents behalf which children make a good match. The progress of councils in recruiting more adopters will be overseen by a new Adoption Leadership Board.

Care plans

Where the local authority wishes to place a child for adoption, it is the duty of the local authority in all care cases to file a care plan. The care plan sets out the local authority's plans for the child's future. The local authority may take the view that adoption is the preferred option. If this is the case, it should advise the court of the likely steps and timescales.

Adoption of children from overseas

There are rules and procedures governing the adoption of children overseas. Anyone wishing to adopt a child from overseas must apply for an eligibility certificate' from a casework team at the Department of Education. The Children and Adoption Act 2006 has introduced new regulations concerning the adoption of children overseas, see summary below.

Who can be adopted?

A person can only be adopted if he or she is under 19 years of age. The application must be made before the child is 18 years old. In practice, if a child is over 12 then removing a child from parents or foster parents may not be in the interests of the child. The local authority will usually look for other alternatives. they must not have been married or have entered into a civil partnership at any time. No application can be made in relation to a child who is under six weeks old.

Who can adopt? Sections 49-51 AC 2002

- A single person

- A person who is the partner of a parent of the person to be adopted
- A married couple
- A couple who have entered into a civil partnership
- An unmarried couple (whether heterosexual or homosexual) who are living as partners in a stable and enduring family relationship
- A prospective adopter must be at least 21 years of age, except a natural parent of a child who must be at least 18
- They must have been habitually resident in the British Isles for at least a year
- They (or one of them if it is a joint application) must be domiciled in the British isles (or habitually resident, together with a fixed intention to live there permanently).

It has to be remembered that under s 51(3) a married person can only adopt on their own if it can be shown that their spouse cannot be found or that they are permanently separated or that their spouses mental or physical condition is such that they are incapable of making an application.

Suitability

ACA 2002 s45 specifies two grounds in assessing the suitability of adopters.

In assessing suitability, the Act specifies:

- suitability and permanence of that relationship (s45(2);
- religious persuasion, racial origin and cultural and linguistic background (s1(5). As stated this section has been repealed in England by the CFA 2014.

In addition to the statutory grounds the adoption agency may have their own criteria. Under the Adoption Act 1976, adoption agencies developed their own views of relevant criteria beyond the bare minimum laid down in statute. Certain types of persons were specifically excluded, for example those with children of their own. Also excluded were those who held certain religious views or no views at all, smokers and those who were overweight. The dominant view was that a child should have a reasonable expectation of parental longevity. The local authority also put an age limit on those who wished to adopt, women at 35 and men at 40. Any person wishing to adopt must undergo an assessment. Adopter assessment details various aspects of the would be adopters home life; language spoken at home; religion; ethnic descent; occupation; current or proposed hours of work; the children in the household; their ethnic descent, type of school that they go to and their relationship to the applicant; family members personalities, interests, experiences; the neighbourhood, its composition, its schools and recreational facilities and public transport. The applicant has to provide a description of where the child will live and its make up. Information on whether the applicant will move house in the future is also required.

The agency will also carry out an assessment of physical and mental health of the proposed adopter.

Matching parents and children
The ACA 2002 also places emphasis on the importance of religious persuasion, racial origin and cultural and linguistic background in the process of matching adoptive parents to children placed for adoption. However, under the 2014 Children and families Act this is not a requirement in England. It is recognised that perfect matching may not always be possible, in fact it will be impossible to match all the variables. In Re C (Adoption: Religious Observance (2002) a child of a mixed race background with Jewish, Irish Roman Catholic and Turkish Cypriot Muslim elements was placed for adoption with a Jewish couple. The guardian for the child issued proceedings arguing that the couple were too Jewish and that the child should be placed in a secular home. The court held that where a child's heritage was very mixed, it

would rarely be possible for it all to be reflected in the identity of the adoptive home.

Regulation and review of decisions

The ACA 2002, s 45, provides for the regulation of agency decisions in respect of suitability. A system of review introduced by the Act ensures that what are called 'qualifying determinations' which are decisions that conclude that a prospective applicant is unsuitable, are subject to review. A system of review is established and decisions about suitability are subject to an independent review. Complaints can be made to the local authority.

Court orders

The orders of the court with regard to adoption are:

- a placement order
- an adoption order
- Post-adoption contact orders

Placement order

A placement order is an order authorising a local authority to place a child for adoption where there is parental consent, or where there is no consent and consent can be dispensed with. The court can only make a placement order where the child is subject to a care order. Conditions for making a care order are met when the child has no parent or guardian and the parents have consented or their consent should be dispensed with.

If parents refuse consent the court can dispense with consent on two statutory grounds. The first ground (s52(2)(a)) is where the parent or guardian cannot be found or is incapable of giving consent. The second ground (s52(2)(b)) is where the welfare of the child requires the consent to be dispensed with.

Adoption order

Under the ACA 2002 s 46, an adoption order is made by the court on an application under s 50 or s 51 giving parental responsibility for the child to adopters. These can be made by the high court, county court or magistrates court. No order can be made without the child attending the hearing, unless special circumstances exist. An adoption order gives parental responsibility to the adopters and the child is treated as if born to the adopters in marriage.

Each parent/guardian must be joined as a respondent as well as the adoption agency or local authority which has care of the child. If the adoption is refused, the child must be returned to the adoption agency within seven days of the order. The court can make a short term order which gives the applicant parental responsibility for two years and not more. Conditions can be attached to the order.

Alternatives to adoption orders

The ACA 2002 s 1(6) requires the court to be satisfied that the order it makes is better than the alternative order or making no order at all. The court is required to consider all alternatives and will look to maintain links with the natural family.

Post -adoption contact orders

Section 9 of the Children and Familes Act 2014 provides for post-adoption contact orders to be made, and allows a court to prohibit contact. Such an order may be made on application by the adopters or the child, or by anyone else with the courts leave.

Adoption by step-parents

The ACA 2000, s 39, provides for adoption by partners of parents. However, it is expected that fewer stepparents will apply for adoption as a parental responsibility order can also infer parental responsibility.

Attempts to speed up the adoption process

The Government has introduced measures in the Children and families Act 2014 to try to speed up the adoption process. Section 2 of the CFA 2014 adds to s 22C of the Children Act 1989 a requirement for a local authority which is considering adoption for a child in care to consider placing the child with foster parents who are already approved as adopters (rather than those yet to undergo the approval process).

In addition, as mentioned s 3 of the 2014 Act repeals in England, but not Wales, the requirement in s 1(5) of the 2002 Act to give consideration to a child's religion, race, culture and language in placing a child for adoption.

Further section 109 of the 2002 Act requires that any court dealing with a placement or adoption application to draw up a timetable to ensure the matter is determined without delay, and to give directions to keep all parties to that timetable.

Discovery and information

The Registrar General is required to keep records so that it is possible to trace the original birth registration of an adopted person. The ACA 2002 provides no absolute right to birth records.

Human rights and genetic identity

Human rights legislation and the UNCRC 1989 reinforce the right of a child to know its genetic identity as follows:

Article 7: Each child should be registered immediately after birth, and has the right from birth to a name, to acquire a nationality, and as far as possible to know and to be cared for by his or her parents;

Article 8: Each child has the right to preserve his or her identity, including nationality, name and family relations, as recognised by law, without unlawful interference.

Article 9: Children should not be separated from their parents against their will, unless competent authorities which are subject to judicial review determine through the applicable legislation and procedures that such separation is necessary for the best interests of the child. All parties to such procedures shall be given the opportunity to participate in the proceedings and make their views known. A child separated from one or both parents has the right to maintain personal relations and direct contact with both parents on a regular basis, unless this is contrary to the child's interests. When separation results from state action such as detention, imprisonment, deportation or exile, the state shall provide essential information about the absent family on request, unless to do so would be detrimental to the child's well-being.

The Children and Adoption Act 2006

This Act is intended to assist in the implementation of the Green Paper *Parental Separation: Children's Needs and Parents' Responsibilities* (Cm 6273), published in July 2004. The Children and Adoption Act 2006 became law in June 2006.

The Act provides the courts with new powers to promote contact and enforce contact orders made under section 8 of the Children Act 1989 ('the 1989 Act'). The Act also makes a number of provisions about intercountry adoption, including a statutory framework for the suspension of intercountry adoption from specified countries where there are concerns about practices in connection with the adoption of children.

Summary of the Act

Part 1 - Orders with respect to children in family proceedings

Part 1 of the Act adds to the powers of the courts when dealing with cases involving contact with children. During the proceedings a court may, even if it does not make a contact order, direct a party to take part in an activity that would promote contact with a child. It may make similar provision by means of a condition in a contact order. The courts' powers in cases involving breach of a contact order are increased by adding:

- a power to make an enforcement order imposing an unpaid work requirement;
- a power to order one person to pay compensation to another for a financial loss caused by a breach. These powers are in addition to their powers as to contempt and their ability to alter the residence and contact arrangements as regards a child. Part 1 also includes provision to reform the courts' existing power to make family assistance orders and imposes a duty on the Children and Family Court Advisory and Support Service (CAFCASS) and Welsh family proceedings officers to carry out risk assessments where they suspect a child is at risk of harm.

Part 2 - Adoptions with a foreign element

12. Part 2 makes provision for the Secretary of State to suspend intercountry adoptions from a country if he has concerns about the practices there in connection with the adoption of children. It also makes other provision for the following other matters relating to intercountry adoption:

- providing a power for the Secretary of State and the National Assembly for Wales to charge a fee to adopters or prospective adopters for services provided in relation to intercountry adoptions;
- preventing an overlap of functions by local authorities where a child is brought into the country for the purposes of intercountry adoption; and
- amending section 83 of the Adoption and Children Act 2002 to make it harder for intercountry adopters to circumvent restrictions on bringing children into the UK.

Part 3 - Miscellaneous and final

Part 3 makes a number of miscellaneous and final provisions, including provision about the operation of orders and regulations made under the Act, and provision about commencement and extent. It also provides for Schedules 2 and 3, which make provision for minor and consequential amendments and repeals, to have effect.

Territorial extent

Part 1 of the Act extends only to England and Wales. Part 2 extends to England, Wales and Northern Ireland. The Annex contains a summary of the effects on the powers of the National Assembly for Wales.

****

Ch.11

Protection of Children and the Resolution of Disputes

Section 8 of the Children Act 1989 outlines the orders which can be issued by the court with respect to resolving disputes over children. These orders have become known as **Section 8 Orders**.

Notably, these orders are not granted to the local authority. They are for the resolution of family disputes and are aspects of private law.

The Children Act makes it very clear that these orders are not to be sought as the first option and that all efforts should be made to resolve problems voluntarily. Only when there has been no resolution of the matter should these Court Orders be sought, and only then if they will be of positive benefit to the child.

Originally, four different types of Order were laid down in Section 8. With the advent of the Children and Families Act 2014, these were reduced to three, Contact Orders and Residence Orders being replaced by Child Arrangements Orders:

Child Arrangements Orders
Prohibited Steps Orders
Specific Issue Orders

"Section 8 Orders" refer to any of the above orders, or any order varying or discharging such an order.

A "child arrangements order" gives the Court's decision in terms of an order regulating arrangements concerning with whom a child is to live, spend time or otherwise have contact and when a child is to live, spend time or otherwise have contact with any person.

A "prohibited steps order" gives the Court's decision in terms of restricting the exercise of full parental responsibility without specific consent of the court, where it is believed that this responsibility would be abused and not exercised to the benefit of the child. For instance such an order may prohibit contact with the child except by prior arrangement and under supervision, where there is concern the child may be harmed or abducted.

A "specific issue order" gives the Court's directions in answer to a disagreement that has arisen with regard to the exercising of parental responsibility for the child.

When an application is made to the court for a section 8 order the court takes into account: the nature of the proposed application; the connection the person has to the child; the disruption that could be caused to the child and, if the child is being looked after by the local authority: the local authorities plans for the child's future and the wishes of the child's parents.

More about Child Arrangement Orders

As stated above, from April 22 2014, and following the introduction of the Children and Families Act 2014, Child Arrangements Orders replaced 'Residence Orders' and 'Contact Orders'. The Child Arrangements Programme (the 'CAP') applies where a dispute arises between separated parents and/or families about arrangements concerning children. The CAP is designed to assist families to reach safe and child-focused agreements for their child, where possible out of the court setting.

A Child Arrangements Order decides:

- where a child lives

- when a child spends time with each parent (as well as grandparents and other family members where dispute exists about time spent with grandchildren)

- when and what other types of contact, like phone calls, take place (as well as grandparents and other family members where dispute exists about time spent with grandchildren)

- As Child Arrangements Orders' replace 'residence orders' and 'contact orders', Parents or other family or friends members, such as grandparents, with these orders don't need to re-apply.

- The Children and families Act 2014, repeals s11(4) of the Childrens Act 1989 which provided for shared residence orders that a child was to live with more than one person. It will be possible to make child arrangement orders providing for a child to live with both parents. Shared residence used to be rare, for example in A v A (Minors) (shared residence order) (1994, it was held that a shared order should be made only if there was something unusual about the case. A residence order to one parent with generous contact with the other was to be preferred.

Who can apply for a Child Arrangements Order (Residence Order)?

You can apply for a Child Arrangements Order (Residence) if you:

- Are the child's parent, guardian or special guardian

- Are the child's step parent, who is married to (or is a civil partner of) the child's parent and the child has lived with you as a 'child of the family'

- Are a foster carer approved by Children's Services who has had the child living with you for at least one year

- Are a grandparent, aunt, uncle, sibling or step parent and you have had the child living with you for one year

- Are anyone else and the child has been living with you for at least 3 years (in the last 5 years)

- Have the agreement of anyone who already has a Residence Order on the child; or Children's Services if the child is in care; or

- Everyone else with parental responsibility for the child.

If Social Services are involved
When family circumstances mean that a parent cannot provide a family life for their child, social care professionals are often involved. You may find that they are involved with the case because of:

- S20 Accommodation – (Residence application to avoid care proceedings/stabilise position of child)

- Care order – Grandparent(s) apply for a Child Arrangement Order for Residence as alternative to care order.

- Local Authority is considering Adoption

- Local Authority suggests Grandparent(s) apply for Child Arrangement Order for Residence after child placed with

- them under care order/accommodated

- Social Care Services feel Section 47 threshold (relating to child protection) is not met –

- Grandparent(s) don't agree. Child Arrangement Order for Residence taken out as a protective mechanism

It is important that if you are considering a Child Arrangements Order (Residence) for whatever reason that you make yourself known to social services as they by law (s23 (6) Children Act) have a duty to place child with family or friends unless not 'reasonably practicable' or consistent with the child's welfare.

At this point you can ask for a Family Group Conference (FGC). This is a family-led decision-making process in which the whole family comes together to make plans and decisions for a child who needs a plan that will keep them safe and promote their welfare. Professionals (for example social workers) are involved in setting out their key concerns which must be addressed in the plan at the start of the meeting and agreeing the plan, and help from Children's Services, in the last stage of the meeting. The family are given time to draw up a plan in private which meets the child's needs and addresses the professionals' concerns.

What Court should I contact?

There is now only one Court and that is the Single Family Court, introduced by the Children and families Act 2014. This court acts as a gatekeeper. You will now just issue a family application at your local Family Court who will then decide which level of Judge and which Court will hear the application.

Generally speaking you should apply to the court nearest to where the child lives. However, if you are making an application about a child where there are existing proceedings about that child, you should apply to the same court which is dealing with that case.

Mediation and MIAMS

From April 22nd 2014, anyone applying to the Family Court for assistance in resolving a dispute about parenting or finances following relationship breakdown must undertake compulsory family mediation information meetings (MIAM) and prove to the court that they have done so in the application to the court. (see example at the end of this guidance.) There are some exemptions to this need to attend a MIAM including domestic violence and child abuse. Addresses below.

- National Family Mediation (NFM). **http://www.nfm.org.uk** or ring 0300 4000 636

- Family Mediation Council (FMC)

- www.familymediationcouncil.org.uk

If, after your MIAM, it's considered that mediation is not suitable in your case, the mediator will fill in a form – called the FM – which is now included in the C100 form (see page 19). Signed by a certified mediator, this form confirms that you have attended a MIAM. A court will then allow you to issue proceedings.

This gives the information which will be considered by the court when deciding whether to grant 'leave' to apply (as laid down in the Children Act Part II, s10 (9)).

- What sort of order you wish to apply for.

- Your relationship and personal connection to the child.

- Whether awarding you an order about where a child should live and with whom they should have contact would cause disruption to the child to the extent that they were harmed.

Where the child is 'looked after' by a Local Authority the court must also consider:

- The Local Authority's plans for the child's future.

- The wishes & feelings of the child's parents.

Different types of proceedings

The only way for private individuals to take steps to resolve disputes concerning bringing up a child is for one of them to issue proceeding under the Children's Act. Like the above orders, the Children's Act has greatly simplified dispute resolution. The only exceptions to this relate to wardship and adoption.

Under the Children's Act it is possible to apply for an order appointing a guardian of the child (s 5). An order of this type gives parental responsibility. It is also possible for an unmarried father to apply far an order that gives him parental responsibility. The main type of application possible under the Children Act however, is a section 8 order.

An application for such an order can be made in several ways, either as a "free standing application" or as part of "family proceedings" Section 8 defines "family proceedings" The list includes jurisdictions which used to have their own powers to grant orders relating to upbringing of children, for example the M.C.A. It also includes applications under part one of the Children's Act itself. It should be noted that once family proceedings have commenced, the court can make a section 8 order itself, of its own motion.

Types of applicant

In most cases, it is the parents of the child who are in dispute about its upbringing. However, others with an interest in the child's welfare may also make an application. The Children Act recognises the need for persons other than parents of a child to be able to get orders that relate to the child's upbringing:

Those entitled to apply for any s 8 order:

1. A parent or guardian of the child;
2. A person who has been granted a residence order.

Those entitled to apply for a residence or contact order:

1. A spouse or ex spouse in relation to whom the child is a child of the family;
2. A person with whom the child has lived for at least three years. This need not be continuous as long as the period does not begin more than five years, nor end more than three months before, the making of the application;
3. A person who has the consent of the person in whose favour there is a residence order, if one has been granted, the local authority if the child is in care and in any other case any other person with parental responsibility.

The factors a court must take into account when considering making an order are designed to prevent applications deemed not to be serious and also possibly injurious to the child's future well-being. They include the nature of the persons connection with a child (s 10 (9)).

Protection of Children-Local Authorities
Types of orders available
Before the Children's Act came into being, there were many types of orders available to local authorities which enabled them to offer some form of protection to children. Local authorities could, on passing a specific resolution, assume the role of parent. The Children's Act makes an attempt to get rid of the uncertainty of the old laws. It replaced all the old laws with a new scheme. In addition, local authorities can no longer pass a parental rights resolution. No child may be taken into care without a court order.

The following orders are available:

1.Care orders (s 31);
2. Supervision orders (s 31);
3.The Education supervision order (s 36);
4.The Emergency protection order (s 44);
5.The Child assessment order (s 43).

Care orders
This is an order that commits a child into the care of a local authority. It cannot be made in favour of anyone else. The effect of a care order is that the child in question goes to live in a local authority community home, or with local authority foster parents. The legal effect is that the local authority gains parental responsibility for the child while the order is in force. A care order automatically brings to an end any residence order that exists. But if a parent or guardian has parental responsibility at the time that a care order comes into force, this continues. A care order cannot be made in respect of a child who has

reached 17 (16 if married). It lasts until the age of 18.

Supervision orders

This is an order placing the child under the supervision of a local authority or probation officer. This order does not carry any parental responsibility and there is no power to take a child from his home.

A supervision order can have conditions attached to it as the court sees fit. A supervision order cannot be made in respect of a child who has reached the age of 17 (16 if married). Generally, a supervision order has a life span of one year but can be extended to two years.

Education supervision orders

This is an order placing a child under the supervision of the local education authority.

Emergency protection orders

Orders usually take time to activate. For those children requiring emergency protection the above order is issued. It is an order that empowers the local authority or NSPCC to remove a child from its home and also gives the local authority parental responsibility. Applications can be made ex-parte, without the necessity of informing or involving the child's parents or any other person. In this way, it is possible to obtain the court order very quickly indeed. The order lasts for eight days only and can be extended for a further seven days. After 72 hours, an application for its discharge can be made.

The child assessment order

This order is a new concept, the above replacing orders already in existence. Although a local authority may feel that a child is at risk there are times when it cannot gain access to the child to compile evidence. In the past the local authority could apply for a place of safety order and remove the child immediately from its home. It could also do nothing. The child assessment order has effect for seven days maximum. With such an order it is possible to remove a child from its home. There is no parental responsibility. The intention behind the order is to enable the local authority to assess the child so it can make the necessary arrangements after consideration.

Before the Children's Act came into being, it was possible to make orders giving a local authority the right to intervene in a child's life under a number of jurisdictions, some overlapping. The Children's Act is now the only jurisdiction under which a local authority may act. By section 31 (4) an application for a care order or a supervision order can be made on its own or within family proceedings as defined by section 8 (3) of the Act. Applications for education supervision orders, emergency protection orders and child assessment orders have to made alone.

Categories of applicants for orders are limited to the following:

Care orders, supervision orders and child assessment orders-only a local authority or NSPCC may apply. Education supervision orders-only a local education authority may apply. Emergency protection orders-only a local authority may apply. In place of previous powers to make different orders, the court now has intermediate powers under section 37. Where a court is dealing with family proceedings in which a question relating to the welfare of a child arises, it may direct the local authority to carry out investigations. The local authority must respond and decide what order should be applied for. If the local authority decides not to apply for an order the court cannot make it do so, although this fact must be reported to the court.

Grounds on which a court will grant an order (s 31(2))

A court has to be satisfied of the following before granting an order:
(a) that the child has suffered or is likely to suffer significant harm;
(b) that the harm or likelihood of harm is attributable to the care given to the child, or likely to be given to him if the order were not made or the child being beyond parental control. Proof of the ground in section 31(2) only entitles accoutre to grant a care or supervision order. The court does not have to grant such an order. The grounds in this section

are referred to as "threshold" grounds.

In relation to education and supervision orders, the court has to be satisfied that the child is of compulsory school age and not being properly educated. To obtain an emergency protection order, the local authority must demonstrate the following:

(a) a local authority must show that the enquiries are being frustrated and that access to the child is required urgently;
(b) the NSPCC must show that it has reasonable cause to suspect that the child is in danger of suffering significant harm;
(c) any other applicant must show that there is reasonable cause to believe that the child is likely to suffer significant harm if he is not removed from the home.

As with the other orders, applications for emergency protection orders are subject to section 1 of the Act. For child assessment orders, the court has to be satisfied that:

(a) the applicant has reasonable cause to suspect that the child is suffering or likely to suffer significant harm;
(b) this can only be determined by an assessment of the child's health or development;
(c) it is not likely that an assessment can be made without an order.

Again, applications for this order are subject to section 1 of the Children Act.

Parental contact

By section 34 of the Act a local authority is under a duty to allow reasonable contact between a child in care and his parents. If there is any dispute on the reasonableness of contact, the court can regulate. In limited circumstances, a local authority can refuse to allow contact for up to seven days. By section 43, if a child is to be kept away from home during the currency of the child assent order, the order must contain directions for such contact between the child and other persons as the court thinks fit.

By section 44, an applicant who is granted such an order is placed under a duty to allow reasonable contact between child and parents.

Wardship

Wardship is the means by which the family court fulfils its jurisdiction of protection of children. When a child becomes a ward of court, the court controls its upbringing by a series of orders.

The Children and Young Persons Act 2008

The Children's and Young Persons Act received royal assent in November 2008. The purpose of the Act was to reform the statutory framework for the care system by implementing the proposals in the June 2007 white paper, Care Matters: Time for Change, that require primary legislation. It includes provision in relation to private fostering, child death notification to Local Safeguarding Children's Boards and the secretary of state's powers to conduct research and applications for the discharge of emergency protection orders. The Act also amends the public law framework for safeguarding and promoting children's welfare through amendments to the services that are to be provided to support children and their families and the procedures to protect children who are at risk of suffering harm. The key legislation to be amended is The Children's Act 1989, The Children (Leaving Care) Act 2000, The Adoption and Children Act 2002 and the Children Act 2004.

In summary, the Act:

- enables local authorities to delegate their functions in relation to looked after children to providers of social work services;
- prevents local authorities from placing looked after children outside their area unless it is consistent with a child's welfare and the care provision is not available within the LA area;
- prevents local authorities from moving a looked after child from a local authority placement with a LA foster parent or a children's

home, unless it was decided to do so as a consequence of a statutory review of a child's case;

- amends LA duties relating to the appointment of the Independent Reviewing Officer;
- extends the duties of local authorities to appoint an independent person to visit, befriend and advise any looked after child if it is in the child's best interests;
- places a duty on governing bodies of maintained schools to appoint a member of staff to be responsible for promoting the educational achievement of registered looked after pupils;
- extend the local authorities duties to appoint a personal advisor and keep the pathway plan under regular review for young people who are former relevant children and who start or resume a programme of education and training after the age of 21 but under the age of 25;
- requires a local authority to pay a bursary to a former relevant child (i.e. a care leaver) who goes on to higher education;
- extends the powers of local authorities to make cash payments to children in need and their families;
- makes provision to enable registration authorities to issue compliance notices to children's home providers who are failing to meet national standards and to impose a notice to prevent new admissions to establishments where this is deemed appropriate;
- amend the procedures around reporting child deaths;

There are other amendments in the legislation, the above of which are key.

The Act is in five parts:

- Part 1 clauses 1-6 deals with arrangements for the provision of social work services
- Part 2 clauses 7-28 principally amends the Children's Act 1989 Part 3 in respect of local authority duties when providing

135

accommodation for looked after children; the power to establish a national IRO service; arrangements for local authorities representatives to visit children and young people living away from home; the appointment of independent visitors to looked after children; extends the entitlements of former looked after children; amends the CSA through the enforcement of national standards in children's homes; extends the powers of local authorities to make cash payments to children in need and their families; and removes the restrictions on courts to hear applications to discharge an emergency protection order.

■ Part 3 Clauses 29-31 amends the Children's Act 1989 Sch 2 to allow for an independent review of the suitability of local authority foster parents.

■ Part 4 clauses 32-34 makes amendments to the Children's Act 1989 Part 1 in relation to residence orders and special guardianship orders.

■ Part 5 clauses 35-40 contains general and financial provisions.

International Child Abduction
Section 1(2) Child Abduction Act 1984 makes it an offence for a person connected with the child to remove a child under 16 from the UK (without consent from certain specified people).

Parent child abduction can take two forms: Removal without consent; Retention once consent has expired. The difference between removal and retention was clarified in the House of Lords in Re H: Re S (Abduction; Custody Rights 1991). Removal is 'when a child, which has previously been in the state of its habitual residence, is taken away across the frontier of that state'. Retention is 'where a child, which has previously been for a limited period of time outside the state of its habitual residence, is not returned on the expiry of such limited period'.

The Child Abduction Act 1984 creates a range of criminal offences to deal with the full range of potential child abductions. Section 1(1) deals with international parent-child abduction. This states that:

o A person connected with a child under 16 years of age commits an offence if they take or send the child out of the United Kingdom without the appropriate consent.

A person is 'connected with a child' if they are a parent or guardian or special guardian of the child; anyone named in a child arrangements order as the person with whom the child will live or who has custody of the child; and if a child's parents were not married to each other at the time of his birth, there are reasonable grounds for believing that the man is the father of the child.

Section 1(3) defines the 'appropriate consent' in relation to a child as:

- the consent of each of the child's mother, father (if he has parental responsibility for him); a guardian; anyone who the child lives with under a child arrangements order or anyone who has custody of the child; or
- the leave of the court granted under Part 11 Children Act 1989, or the leave of any court which has awarded the custody of the child to anyone.

Section 1(4) and s 1(5) provide for defences to a s 1(1) charge.

A person does not commit an offence if he has a child arrangements order in his favour providing for the child to live with him *and* he takes or sends the child out of the UK for less than a month, unless he does so in breach of an order under Part 11 of the Children Act 1989. Section 1(5) elaborates on this.

****

Ch.12

Making a Will

The main principle underlying any will is that, if you have possessions, own property etc then you need to organise a will which will ensure that chosen people benefit after your death.

In the majority of cases, a person's affairs are relatively uncomplicated and should not involve the use of a solicitor.

There are certain basic rules to be followed in the formation of a will and if they are then it should be legally binding.

The only inhibiting factor on the disposal of your assets will be any tax liability following death, which will be dealt with later in this book. There are a number of other factors to consider, however:

- Age of person making a will

A will made by anyone under the age of eighteen, known as a minor, will not be valid unless that person is a member of the services (armed forces) and is on active service.

- Mental health considerations

A will formed by a person, who was insane at the time of writing, will not be valid. Mental illness in itself is not a barrier to creating a will, as long as proof can be shown that the person was not insane at the time of writing.

Subsequent mental illness, following the formation of a will, will not be a barrier to a will's validity.

Definition of insanity

Insanity, or this particular condition, will normally apply to anyone certified as such and detained in a mental institution. In addition, the Mental Health Act covers those in " a state of arrested or incomplete development of mind which includes sub-normality of intelligence and is of such a nature or degree that the patient is incapable of living an independent life or guarding against serious exploitation.

In any situation where there is doubt as to a persons capabilities then it is always best to have any will validated by an expert. This applies to anyone, not just those classified as insane.

The main point of any will is that, in the final analysis, a court would have to be satisfied that the contents of the will are genuine, there has not been any attempt whatsoever to alter the contents or to influence that persons mind. The person writing the will must have fashioned its contents with no outside interference.

Unfortunately, the history of the production of people's last will and testament is littered with greedy and unscrupulous persons who wish to gain from another's demise. It is necessary to be careful!

Making a will

The main reason for making a will is to ensure that you make the choice as to who you leave your possessions, and not the state. You can also impose any specific conditions you want in your will. For example, you can impose age conditions or conditions relating to the need to perform certain duties before benefiting.

If you do not make a will then, on your death, the law of intestacy will apply to the disposal of your estate. You will have had no say and certain criteria are applied by the state, which will take responsibility. In the circumstances described above, after costs such as funeral and administration of other aspects of death, an order of preference is established, as follows:

- Your spouse, which is your husband or wife/civil partner

- Any children you may have. This includes all children, whether by marriage, illegitimate or adopted.
- Parents
- Brothers and sisters
- Half brothers or sisters
- Grandparents
- Uncles and aunts
- Uncles and aunts (half blood)

It is the law of intestacy that if any of the above, in that order, die before the person who is the subject of intestacy, then their children will automatically benefit in their place.

There are conditions which will affect the above order of beneficiaries:

- If the spouse/civil partner of a person is still living and there are no surviving children, parents, brothers or sisters or any of their offspring living then the spouse/CP will benefit solely
- If the spouse/CP is still living and there is children, the estate will be divided along the following lines:

The spouse/CP will take all the personal items and up to £75,000 if money is involved. This will be augmented by interest on the money from the date of death. There will be a life interest in half of the residue of the estate. This means use as opposed to ownership. In the case of money it relates to interest on capital only and not the capital itself;

Children (equal shares) Half the residue of the estate plus the other half on the death of the spouse.

If the spouse/CP is still alive, there are no children but there are other relatives, such as parents, brothers and sisters and their children the following rules apply:

The spouse/CP will have all the personal items and up to £125000 if it is available, interest on money and half the residue of the estate;

Parents will receive half the residue or, if there are no parents alive then brothers and sisters will, in equal shares, keep half the residue.

By law, the spouse/CP is entitled to carry on living in the matrimonial home after death. The matrimonial home is defined as the place where he or she had been living at the time of death.

If there is no spouse/CP living but there are children then the estate will be divided equally between them. This will occur when they are over the age of eighteen or marry, whichever occurs first.

If there is no spouse/CP and no children but there are parents, then the estate will be divided equally between them. If there is no spouse, no children and no parents, then the estate will be divided equally between brothers and sisters. If there are no brothers and sisters then half brothers and sisters. If none, grandparents. If not, uncles and aunts and if none to half blood uncles and aunts. As can be seen, the law of intestacy tries to ensure that at least someone benefits from a person possessions on death. There is a ranking order and in most cases there would be someone to benefit. There are certain categories of person who fall outside of the law of intestacy, even though there may have been some connection in the past:

Divorced and separated Persons
There is no right of entitlement whatsoever for a divorced person to benefit from an estate on death. This right ceases from the decree absolute. If a separation order is granted by a divorce court then there is no entitlement to benefit. If the separation is informal and there is separate habitation or a Magistrates court order has been granted for separation then there is normal entitlement.

Cohabitation
The law of intestacy dictates that, if you were living with someone, but not married, at the time of death, then that person has no direct claim to the estate. However, in practice this operates somewhat differently

and there is a law, Provision for Family and Dependants Act 1975 under which cohabitees can claim. We will be discussing this a little later.

Although anyone has a right to have their estate distributed in accordance with the law of intestacy it is highly inadvisable. It is better at all time to ensure that you have complete control over where your money goes. It may be that you do not wish immediate family to benefit over others and that you wish to leave all your money to a particular favoured person or to an institution. This can only be achieved by personalising your will and remaining in control of what happens after your death.

The decision to make a will

It is essential that you make a will as soon as possible. If you leave it, there is a chance that you may never get round to doing it and may be reliant upon the state doing it for you. There is also the chance that you will leave a situation where people start to contest your possessions, fight amongst each other and fall out.

There are many things to consider when you decide to produce a will. As a person gets older, chances are that he or she will become wealthier. Savings grow, endowments increase, insurance policies become more valuable, property is purchased and so on. A bank balance in itself is no indicator of worth, as there are many other elements which add up to wealth. Changes in personal circumstances often justify the need to make a will.

- Ownership of property
- Children
- Marriage or remarriage
- Employment
- Illness
- Divorce and separation
- Increase in personal wealth, such as an inheritance

Ownership of property

Ownership of property usually implies a mortgage. If you are wise it will also imply life insurance to at least the value of the property. It is very prudent to make a will which specifies exactly to whom the property will be left. As we have seen, the law of intestacy provides for the decision if you do not have a will.

Children

As we have seen, under the law of intestacy, any children you have will benefit after your death. However, it is very sensible, under a will, to specify how and when they will benefit. It could be that you may let someone else make that decision later on. Whatever, you should make it very clear in your will.

Marriage or remarriage

The most important point to remember is that marriage or remarriage will automatically revoke the provisions of any former will, although this is not the case in Scotland. Therefore, when marrying you should make certain that your will is up to date and that you have altered the provisions. In short, you should amend your will, or produce a new will in order to outline clearly what you want your new partner to have.

Employment

You should be very aware that certain types of employment carry greater risks than others. This will necessitate producing a will as soon as possible as if you are in a high-risk category then you need to ensure that those nearest you are catered for.

Illness

Illness is something that none of us want but cannot avoid if it decides to strike. No matter how healthy you are you should take this into account when considering putting together a will. In addition, some people have a family history of illness and chances are that they too could suffer. Therefore illness is a very real motivator for producing a will.

Divorce and separation
The law of intestacy states that if you die your divorced spouse loses all rights to your estate. You may not want this to happen and make provisions in your will. Although children of any marriage will benefit it could be that you may wish to make slightly different provisions for different children.

Increase in personal wealth
Financial success, and inheritance will increase your wealth and inevitably make you estate more complicated. It is absolutely essential to ensure that you have a will and that you are updating that will regularly to take into account increased assets.

The provisions of a will
Having considered some of the many reasons for producing a will, it is now necessary to look at exactly what goes into a will. Essentially, the purpose of a will is to ensure that everything you have accumulated in your life is disposed of in accordance with your own desires. The main areas to consider when formulating a will are:

- Money you have saved, in whatever form
- Any buildings (property) you have
- Any land you have
- Any insurance policies you have. This is of utmost importance
- Any shares you may own
- Trusts set up
- Any other personal effects

Money you have saved
Money is treated as part of your wider estate and will automatically go to those named as the main beneficiaries. However, you might wish to

make individual bequests to other people outside your family. These have to be specified. When including any provisions in your will relating to money, you should be very clear about the whereabouts of any saving accounts or endowments, premium bonds etc. Life becomes very difficult if you have left sums of money but there is no knowledge of the whereabouts of this. Inevitably, solicitors have to be employed and this becomes very expensive indeed.

Property
It is necessary to make provisions for any property you have. If you are the sole owner of a property then you can dispose of it as you wish. Any organisation with a superior interest would take an interest, particularly if there are mortgages outstanding. It is important to remember that if you are a joint owner of a property, such as a joint tenancy, then on death this joint ownership reverts to the other joint owner, bringing it into sole ownership.

Leasehold property can be different only in so much as the executor of an estate will usually need permission before assigning a lease. This can be obtained from the freeholder.

Land
Although the same principles apply to land as to property, indeed often the two are combined, in certain circumstances land may be owned separately. In this case the land and everything on it can be left in the will.

Insurance policies
The contents of any insurance policy needs to be checked carefully. In certain cases there are restrictions on who can benefit on death. Particular people may be specified and you have no alternative but to let such people benefit, even though your own circumstances may have changed. If there are no restrictions then you can bequeath any money as you see fit.

Shares

Shares can normally be bequeathed in a will as anything else. However, depending on the type of share, it is just possible that there may be restrictions. One such situation is where shares are held in a private company and there may be a buy back clause.

Trusts

Trusts can be set up for the benefit of family and friends. However, a trust, by its very nature is complex as the law dealing with trusts is complex. It is absolutely essential, if you are considering setting up a trust to get specialist advice.

Personal effects

Although you are perfectly entitled to leave specific items of personal effects in your will, such legacies are separate from those of other possessions such as money or land.

The law recognises that in some cases there may not be enough money to pay expenses related to your death. Any money owed will be retrieved from any financial gifts you have outlined. However, personal effects cannot be touched if you have clearly identified these in your will. This includes items of value such as jewellery.

It is not enough to be general on this point. You must specify exactly what it is you are leaving and to whom. Remember, certain gifts will be taxable.

The funeral

It is common practice to include such matters as how you wish to be buried, in what manner and the nature of the ceremony, in your will. You should discuss these arrangements with your next of kin in addition to specifying them in your will as arrangements may be made for a funeral before details of a will are made public. Another way is to detail your wishes in a letter and pass this on to your executor to ensure that the details are known beforehand. There is no reason why any of your instructions should not be carried out, subject to the law.

However, your executor can override your wishes if necessary and expedient. You can, in addition, make known your wishes for maintenance of your grave after your death. Agreement of the local authority, or relevant burial authority must be sought and there is no obligation on them to do this. In addition, there is a time limit of 99 years in force.

The use of your body after death

It could be that you have decided to leave your body for medical research or donate your organs. This can be done during your final illness, in writing or in front of a minimum of two witnesses. You should contact your local hospital or General Practitioner about this, they will supply you with more details.

Making a recital

A recital consists of a statement at the end of your will which explains how and why you have drawn up a will in the way you have. This is not commonly done but sometimes may be necessary, especially if you have cut people out of your will but do not intend to cause confusion or hurt.

Recitals are sometimes necessary in order to clarify a transfer of authority to others on your death. This could be in business for example. In addition, you may wish to recognise someone's contribution to your life, for example a long serving employee or a particular friend.

Making provisions in your will

Who to name

When including persons, or organisations, in your will it is better to form a separate list right at the outset.

Naming individuals in your will

There are certain criteria which apply when naming individuals in a will, although in principle you can name who you want. Any person considered an adult, i.e. over 18, can benefit from your will. However, if a person cannot be traced within a time period of seven years after being named, or dies before you, then the amount left in your will to that person is included in what is known as the residue of your estate, what is left after all bequests. You can also make a bequest in your will to cover that eventuality, that is for another named person to benefit in his or her place.

If the bequest is to your own children or any other direct descendant and they die before you then the gift will automatically go to their children, unless there is something to the contrary in your will. In addition, if you make a gift to two or more people and one dies then that share is automatically passed to the other (joint owner).

Children

You are entitled to leave what you want in your will to children whether they are illegitimate or stepchildren. Stepchildren should be stipulated in your will. If children are under 18 then it will be probably necessary to leave property such as land, in trust for them until they reach 18 or any other age stated in the will. No child under 18 can be a trustee. Those people who are not British citizens, i.e. foreigners can benefit from your will in the same way as anyone else.

The only real restriction to this is if there is a state of war between your own country and theirs, in which case it will be necessary to wait until peace is declared.

Mental illness

There is nothing currently in law which prevents a person suffering mental illness from receiving a bequest under a will. Obviously, depending on the state of mind of that person it could be that someone may have to accept the gift and take care of it on the persons behalf.

Bankruptcy

If a person is either bankrupt or facing bankruptcy then if that person receives a gift there is a chance that it could end up in the hands of a creditor. To avoid this happening you can establish a protective trust which will enable the person in receipt of the gift to enjoy any interest arising from the gift during a specific time.

Animals

It is possible to leave money to animals for their care and well-being. There is a time limit involved for receipt of the money, which is currently a period of 21 years.

Groups

There is no problem legally with leaving money and other gifts to groups or organisations. However, it is necessary to ensure that the wording of the will is structured in a certain way. It is necessary to understand some of the legislation concerning charities, in order that your bequest can be deemed charitable.

Leaving money/gifts to charities

Many people leave bequests to charity. Major charities often give advice to individuals and other organisations on how to do that. Smaller charities can pose a problem as they may not be as sound and as well administered as larger ones. It is best to stipulate an alternative charity in the event of the smaller one ceasing to operate. If for whatever reason you bequest cannot be passed on to the group concerned then it will be left in the residue of your estate and could be liable to tax. There are a number of causes which might be deemed as charitable. These are:

- Educational causes
- Help for the community
- Animal welfare
- Help for the elderly

- Disabled
- Religious groups
- Sick, such as hospices

In the event of making a bequest to a charitable cause, it is certain that you will need expert advice, as with the setting up of trusts.

Preparing a will

One of the key rules is that there should be nothing in your will that can be ambiguous or open to interpretation. It is essential to ensure that your intentions are crystal clear. It will probably be necessary to get someone else to look at your will to ensure that it is understood by others.

Preparation of will

A will can of course be rewritten. However, it is very important indeed to ensure that you have spent enough time in the initial preparation stages of your will as it could be enacted at any time, in the event of sudden death. If your possessions are numerous then it is highly likely that the preparation stage will be fairly lengthy as the dividing up will take more thought. This gets more complicated depending on your other circumstances, such as whether you are married or single, have children, intend to leave money to organizations, etc.

You need to make a clear list of what it is you have in order to be able to achieve clarity in your will. For example, property and other possessions will take in any buildings and land you own plus money in various accounts or other forms of saving. In addition there could be jewelry and other valuables to take into account. It is necessary to quantify the current value of these possessions. It is also necessary to balance this out by making a list of any outstanding loans/mortgages or other debts you may have. Funeral costs should come into this. It is essential that you do not attempt to give away more than you actually have and also to deduce any tax liabilities from the final amount after debts. The wording of any will is always done with tax liability in mind.

Listing those who will benefit from your will

Making a list of beneficiaries is obviously necessary, including all groups, individuals and others who will benefit. With each beneficiary you should list exactly what it is that you bequeath. If a trust is necessary, then note this and note down the name of proposed trustees. These persons should be in agreement before being named. Contact any charities that will benefit. They can supply you with a legacy clause to include in your will.

The most important point, at this stage, is that you ensure that what you are leaving does not exceed the estate and that, if liable for tax, then there is sufficient left over to meet these liability.

Make a note of any recitals that you wish to include in your will and exactly what you wish to say.

The choice of an executor of your will

The job of any executor is to ensure that your will is administered in accordance with the terms therein as far as is legally possible at that time. It is absolutely essential to ask those people is they consent to being an executor. They may well refuse which could pose problems. You can ask friends or family or alternatively you can ask a solicitor or your bank. They will make a charge for this. However, they are much less likely to make a mistake in the execution of the will than an untrained individual. They will charge and this should be provided for. If you do choose to appoint an untrained executor, then it is good policy to appoint at least two in order to ensure that there is an element of double checking and that there are enough people to fulfill the required duties.

The presentation of your will

You can either prepare your will on ordinary sheets of paper or used specially prepared forms which can be obtained from stationers or book shops. Bookshops will usually sell "will packs" which take you through the whole preparation stage, from contemplation to completion.

Try to avoid handwriting your will. If it cannot be read then it will be invalid. You should always try to produce it on a word processor or typewriter. This can be more easily altered at any time.

The advantage of using a pre-printed form is that it has all of the required phrases on it and you just fill in the blanks. It just may be that you are not in the position to write your will, as you may be one of the considerable numbers of people who cannot read or write in this country. In this case, you can get someone else to write it for you although it is essential that you understand the contents. Get someone else, independent of the person who wrote it to read it back to you to ensure that the contents reflect your wishes.

Safekeeping of a will

A will must always be kept safe and should be able to be located at the time of your death. You may spend a great deal of time on your will. However, if it cannot be found then it will be assumed that you have not made one.

Wills and the courts

Courts have wide powers to make alterations to a persons will, after that persons death. It can exercise these powers if the will fails to achieve the intentions of the person who wrote it, as a result of a clerical error or a failure to understand the instructions of the person producing the will. In addition, if mental illness can be demonstrated at the time of producing the will then this can also lead to the courts intervening.

In order to get the courts to exercise their powers, an application must be made within six months of the date on which probate is taken out. If gifts or other are distributed and a court order is made to rectify the will then all must be returned to be distributed in accordance with the court order.

If any part of a persons will appears to have no meaning or is ambiguous then the court will look at any surrounding evidence and the testators intention and will rectify the will in the light of this evidence.

Former spouse

There is one main condition under which a former spouse can claim and that is that they have not remarried. In addition, such a claim would be for only essential maintenance which would stop on remarriage. There is one key exception, that is that if your death occurs within a year of divorce or legal separation, your former spouse can make a claim.

Child of the deceased

As the above, any claim by children can only be on the basis of hardship.

Stepchildren

This includes anyone treated as your own child and supported by you, including illegitimate children or those conceived before, but not born till after, your death. The claim can only cover essential maintenance.

Dependants

This covers a wide range of potential claimants. Maintenance only is payable. There needs to be evidence of full or partial maintenance prior to death. Such support does not have to be financial, however.

There is another situation where the court can change a will after your death. This relates directly to conditions that you may have imposed on a beneficiary in order to receive a gift which are unreasonable. If the court decides that this is the case, that particular condition becomes void and does not have to be fulfilled.

If the condition involved something being done before the beneficiary receives the gift then the beneficiary does not receive the gift. If the condition involved something being done after the beneficiary received the gift then the beneficiary can have the gift without condition.

If the beneficiary does not receive the gift, as in the above, then either the will can make alternative provision or the gift can form part of the residue of the estate. Unreasonable conditions can be many, one such being any condition that provides reason or incentive to break up a marriage, intention to remain celibate or not to remarry or one that separates children. There are others which impinge on religion, general behaviour and crime. An unreasonable condition very much depends on the perception of the beneficiary and the perception of the courts. A beneficiary can lose the right to a bequest, apart from any failure to meet conditions attached to a bequest. Again, a court will decide in what circumstance this is appropriate. Crime could be a reason, such as murder, or evidence of coercion or harassment of another person in pursuit of selfish gain.

Probate

Probate simply means that the executor's powers to administer the estate of a dead person have been officially confirmed. A document called a "Grant of Representation" is given which enables those administering the estate to gain access to all relevant information, financial or otherwise concerning the person's estate.

Although anyone charged under a will to act on behalf of the dead persons estate has automatic authority to represent, there are certain cases where evidence of probate is required. If no will exists or no executors have been appointed, then it will be necessary to obtain "letters of administration" which involves a similar procedure.

Under common law, probate has a number of objectives. These are:

- To safeguard creditors of the deceased
- To ensure reasonable provision is made for the deceased's dependants
- To distribute the balance of the estate in accordance with the intentions of the person whose will it is.

One of the key factors affecting the need to obtain probate is how much money is involved under the terms of a will. Where the sums involved are relatively small then financial institutions and other organisations will not normally want to see evidence of probate. However, it should be remembered that no on is obliged to release anything relating to a dead persons estate unless letters of administration or documents of probate can be shown. Those responsible for administering the estate must find out from the organisations concerned what the necessary procedure is.

Applying for probate

Where a will is in existence and executors have been appointed then any one of the named people can make the application. Where a will is in existence but no executors have been appointed, then the person who benefits from the whole estate should make the application. This would be the case where any known executor cannot or will not apply for probate.

Where there is no will in existence then the next of kin can apply for probate. There is an order of priority relating to the application:

- The surviving spouse
- A child of the deceased
- A parent of the deceased
- A brother or sister of the deceased
- Another relative of the deceased

The person applying for probate must be over eighteen. 'Children' includes any that are illegitimate. If a child dies before the deceased then one of his or her children can apply for probate.

Application for probate

This can be done through any probate registry or office. There is usually one in every main town and any office in any area will accept the application. If you are writing then you should always address your correspondence to a registry and not an office. You can also contact the Probate Registry and Inheritance Tax Helpline 0845 302 0900 or visit the website www.justice.gov.uk which deals with matters of probate.

What needs to be done next

The next of kin should register the death with the register of Births and Deaths. A death certificate will be supplied and copies of the death certificate which will need to be included to various institutions and organisations.

A copy of the will has to be obtained. The whereabouts should be known to the executors. The executor should then take a copy of the will in case the original is lost. The executor will need to obtain full details of the dead persons estate, including all property and other items together with a current valuation. It is possible that on many of the less substantial items a personal valuation can be made. It should however, be as accurate as possible.

In the case of any bank accounts a letter should be sent by the executor to the bank manager, stating that he is the executor and giving full details of the death. Details should be requested concerning the amount of money in the dead persons account(s) together with any other details of valuables lodged with the bank. The bank manager may be able to pass on information concerning holdings in stocks and shares. If share certificates are held then a valuation of the shares at time of death should be requested.

In the case of insurance policies, the same procedure should be followed. A letter should be sent to the insurance company requesting details of policies and amounts owed or payable.

In the case of National Savings Certificates the executor should write to the Savings Certificate Office in Durham and ask for a list of all certificates held, date of issue and current value. In the case of Premium Bonds a letter should be sent to the Bond and Stock Office in Lancashire Giving name and date of death. Premium Bonds remain in the draw for 12 months after death, so they can be left invested for that time or cashed in when probate has been obtained. Form SB4 (obtained from any post office) is used to inform of death and obtain repayment of most government bonds.

In the case of property, whatever valuation is put on a property the Inland revenue can always insist on its own valuation. If there is a mortgage, the executor should write to the mortgagee asking for the amount outstanding at the time of death.

The above procedure should be followed when writing to any one or an organisation, such as a pension fund, requesting details of monies owed to the dead person.

Debts owed by the person

The executor will need to compile a list of debts owed by the dead person as these will need to be paid out of the estate. These debts will include all money owed, loans, overdrafts, bills and other liabilities. If there is any doubt about the extent of the debts then the executor can advertise in the London Gazette and any newspaper which circulates in the area where the estate is situated. Efforts also have to be made to locate creditors outside of advertising. The advert will tell creditors that they have to claim by a certain date after which the estate will be administered having obtained probate.

Funeral expenses should be quantified and a letter should be sent to HM Revenue and Customs to determine the income tax position of the dead person.

Finally

The executor obtains the application form, decides where he or she wishes to be interviewed, send the completed form together with the death certificate and the original will to the Probate Registry and then attends for an interview.

****

Index